CHEF SEEMA .

Magical Mumbai Flavours

A Passionate Food Love Story

Dear Jacqueline & Tony
 I am so happy you enjoyed
the whole cookery lesson. I do
hope you love and enjoy
cooking magical dishes using
this cookery book.
Stay Blessed
Seema Dalvi x x

AUSTIN MACAULEY PUBLISHERS™
LONDON • CAMBRIDGE • NEW YORK • SHARJAH

A CIP catalogue record for this title is available from the British Library.

ISBN 9781398460522 (Paperback)
ISBN 9781398460539 (Hardback)
ISBN 9781398460546 (ePub e-book)

www.austinmacauley.com

First Published 2022
Austin Macauley Publishers Ltd
1 Canada Square
Canary Wharf
London
E14 5AA

Acknowledgements

Where should I start with this?

My first acknowledgement is to my soulmate, Krish, who always stands next to me, understands me, is there for me and never gives up on me. Thank you, Krish, for your love, support, advice and everything you do.

My mum, the best cook in the world – who let me help her in the kitchen from a very early age. You always have been encouraging, even though my chapatis were wonky, my noodles had too much oil and my daal had too much water when I was learning how to cook.

My dad – who always tried and tasted anything and everything I cooked without any hesitation and praised me like anything. I still miss your pilau, though!

My nan – who was the best chef in the world and whose presence I always feel around me when I am cooking her dishes.

Aai (mother-in-law) – who accepted me the way I was and taught me a lot of Maharashtrian dishes, especially the fish dishes. I do miss you and miss our conversations. I wish I could show you what your daughter-in-law has achieved during this world pandemic.

My children Aarya and Aadhritt – who have been real cheerleaders for me and have always been there for their mum. I am so proud of you both.

My sisters-in-law – who are my best friends too. Thank you for all your advice and support.

Michael Shepherd from Just by Michael for photography and creative suggestions.

Marie Diamond – You have been a guiding angel for me. Thank you for your advice throughout.

Simon and Carla – Thank you both for being a huge part of my journey and for all your support. You both mean a lot to me.

Moo, Debbie, Elizabeth, Julia, Becky and Julie – for all your support regarding this book and Dalvi's Restaurant.

Contents

About This Book 9

A Little Bit About Me 11

The Indian Way of Eating Meals 13

Techniques and Tips to Remember Before You Start with these Recipes 16

More Than Just Ingredients 23

Understanding the Diversity of Culinary Heritage 36

Is Indian Food Authentic? 37

STREET FOOD FROM MUMBAI 39

   Vada (or Wada) Pav 41

   Anda Bhurji Pav 43

   Mumbai Cheese Masala Toast Sandwich 47

   Pav Bhaji 49

   Vegetable Schezwan (or Sichuan) Noodles 53

APPETIZERS, SNACKS AND SOUPS 55

   Aloo Tikki Chaat 57

   Vegetable Samosas Triangle and Potalis 59

   Railway Cutlets 67

   Indo-Mexican Aloo Chaat 71

   Mulligatawny Chicken Soup 73

   Spinach Lentil Carrot Soup 77

   Tomato Shorba 79

   Masala Chicken Chimichanga (or Chivichanga) with Homemade Salsa 83

   Rava Prawns 87

   Fish Cakes 89

   Chicken Pakoras 93

   Haryali Chicken Tikka 95

   Turkey Momos 99

Kheema Croquette (or Minced Lamb Cutlets)..........................101

MAIN CURRIES 105

Dalvi's Mixed Vegetable Curry 107

Channa Masala with Potatoes Curry 109

Rajma Chawal 113

Nan's Potato Curry 115

Chicken Curry with a Hint of Spinach..........................119

Dhaba Chicken...121

Butter Chicken 125

Butter Chicken Pizza 129

Malwani (Malvani) Chicken 131

Malai Kadahi Chicken 135

Kerala-Style Lamb Curry 137

Mangshor Jhol Lamb 141

Minced Lamb Kofta Curry...145

Prawn Masala 147

Dalvi's Salmon Curry 151

Red Snapper Fish Saar 153

RICE DISHES..157

Lamb Biryani..158

Chicken Ouzi with Curry Sauce and Raita 163

Vegetable Wild and Basmati Pilau 167

Chickpeas Pilau Rice 169

Masala Mushroom Fried Rice......................................173

Schezwan or Sichuan Fried Rice 175

Pesto Fried Rice 179

Upma 181

BREAD 185

Haryali Pooris 187

Coriander and Garlic Naan 189

Triangle Aloo (Potato) Paneer Parathas.......................193

Masala Laccha Paratha 195

INDIAN DELICACIES AND DESSERTS 201

Masala Chai Crème Brûlée with Almond & Chocolate
Madeleine 203

Date Anjeer (Fig) Barfi 207

Vegan Aamrus Raspberry Cheesecake 209

Almond Pistachio Cupcakes with Shrikhand Frosting 213

Thandai Mousse Dome 215

Pistachio Milk Chocolate Barfi Fudge 219

Orange Chocolate Coconut Ladoo 221

Shahi Tukda 223

SIDES AND CHUTNEYS 225

Whole Moong and Baby Potatoes Salad 226

Apple Beetroot Chutney 227

Mint and Coriander Chutney 228

Red Garlic Chutney 229

Sweet Chilli Red Pepper Chutney 230

Schezwan or Sichuan Chutney 231

Prune, Date and Tamarind Chutney 232

Koshimbir Raita 233

Indian Teas 234

MASALA RECIPES 235

Garam Masala 236

Pastes 238

Pav Bhaji Masala 239

Chaat Masala 241

About This Book

This cookery book showcases my journey through my established yet ever-improving culinary skills and the love affair that led me to cultural fusion. I humbly invite you to embark on this journey and let me take you through recipes I have created – and also recreated – with lots of love, passion and emotion.

I fell in love with Indian cooking at a very young age. The aroma, the seasoning, the masalas, the smell of lightly browned onions, roasted whole spices, and the sputtering sound of cumin seeds, alongside the whistles from the pressure cooker, have always been inviting.

My skills and knowledge have been gratefully acquired from my nan, mother, aunties, friends and their mums, neighbours and my in-laws. I now feel ready to pass the knowledge and the skills to my readers, to my fellow chefs (by passion or by profession) and to those who just love and enjoy the rituals of cooking.

This cookery book is written by someone who has lived and worked in a financial city, Mumbai, and the recipes are a true reflection of how traditional dishes are cooked in many parts of India. Most of my recipes are modified to ensure that they are simple to follow and are achievable. Every recipe has step-by-step guidance, tips, tricks and information on substitute ingredients.

Through this book, I have shared not only mouth-watering traditional regional dishes which have been passed on to me through generations of my family, but also a few dishes with an international touch, i.e. Indo-Mexican, Indo-Chinese, Indo-Italian, Indo-French, Indo-Arabic. The 'fusion' dishes I have shared are very popular at Dalvi's, my restaurant, and I am sure they will become popular in your house, too.

If you are a first-timer in the kitchen in general or with Indian food in particular, I would say: do not worry if your cooked food doesn't look like the food photo shown in this book or tastes far away from what's expected. You should feel proud of yourself for putting in all the efforts to cook that meal by yourself. If you really have the passion, love, and a driving force to cook Indian food and you love the kitchen world, then you have won half the battle. From my personal experience, I can confidently state that you can never cook good-quality meals if you haven't failed in your efforts a few times!

Lastly, this is a must-have cookery book in every kitchen. It doesn't just share good-quality recipes which pair traditional with contemporary ideas and techniques, but also shares the health benefits of many ingredients. This book has recipes from many regions of India and is a true treasure to have.

Happy cooking, everyone!

MAGICAL MUMBAI FLAVOURS

A Little Bit About Me

"I am the master of my fate. I am the captain of my soul."
– William Ernest Henley, 'Invictus'

I am Seema, an award-winning chef and owner of Dalvi's Restaurant. I'm about to take you on my journey from being an underprivileged girl in Mumbai, to a secondary school maths teacher in England, to proudly running my own restaurant – Dalvi's in Poulton-Le-Fylde, Lancashire, England. Allow me to steer you through and let the journey begin.

I was born Seema Sharma, in Mumbai, India to a middle-class "Brahmin" family. The Brahmins are designated as the priestly caste and the traditional occupation of the men is the priesthood. The Brahmins have the highest status of the four social classes. Mumbai, a vibrant Indian city, has always had a special place in my heart. It is the city where I still enjoy street food, the city where I found my dance moves and the city where I found the love of my life.

I was the middle of three children (elder sister, younger brother). My arrival in the world was an unexpected surprise as my parents anticipated a son. Being a girl born in my society was quite tough. During that time, and, even now in some parts of India, sons were, and still are, given greater preference and importance than girls as they are believed to be carrying forward the family lineage. My brother, being the only son, was given greater privilege than my sister and me in everything, including his schooling in an 'English' school. However, I was quite lucky to attend a cheaper version of education based on vernacular teachings.

As a child, food and dance were the strong pillars that held me up, and I was looking forward to pursuing a career in one of those areas, but things didn't go as I hoped and planned. I was allowed to complete my education, including university. However, I was told that after finishing university, I would be expected to marry and have my own family and look after them, as my mother had done; it was the tradition in my family.

I never understood this tradition and as much as my parents imposed, I fought against it. I was rebelling, and my love for meat and seafood (which was forbidden in my family) was growing; at the same time, I was being influenced by my friends from different parts of India. One of the best things about living in a truly cosmopolitan city like Mumbai was that I had friends and neighbours from different parts of India. I was learning about all the country's varieties of cuisine, and I loved it. With pride and pleasure, I have shared some of these most amazing recipes with you in this book.

Another traditional expectation from my family was an arranged marriage – to marry someone I had never met before and to accept them as my life partner. This wasn't something I wanted as a young girl; I had my own dreams and ideals. Expressing my love and feelings wasn't easy, as India's ruthless caste system made a grand entry into my love story. Krish, my now husband, belonged to a warrior caste known as Kashtriya in India. I was from the Brahmin 'varna'; in the traditional pecking order, those from the Kashtriya caste would come below Brahmins. Our flourishing love story would have been objected too, so I anticipated that falling in love with my husband and marrying 'below' myself would not go down well with my family.

Nevertheless, I secretly started dating Krish, but as much as we tried to keep it hidden, the truth came out. This steered my life in a completely different direction, as my dad began looking for a husband for me to put an end to this relationship. Krish worked on ships and this was not approved by my parents. A young love story was slowly shaping up, on enormous trust, yet our movements were watched by my parents. I persuaded my parents to let me start working to earn some money, in the hope that this would help me focus and also take my mind away from living such an orthodox life at home. I worked as an import executive for a reputable company for a few months and enjoyed it to a certain extent as I was earning good money, but the workload was enormous. However, as I didn't get home until late, it did work in my favour as it kept my mind occupied and this helped, as I missed Krish (who by now was a deep-sea sailor) so much. Every attempt I made to persuade my parents to let me marry Krish failed. So, the rebel in me made the bold decision to leave my parents behind, and, with the full blessing of my in-laws, Krish and I got married. I knew I had to dwell on my inner strength – the girl who left her family behind for true love and the first female in my family to marry outside my caste.

A marriage is a beautiful institution and normally brings families together but, in my case, it took a lot of convincing – more than a year – to frame a happy ending. Now both my parents adore Krish, their son-in-law. A true captain who has sailed the seven seas, he has stood by me in every storm, every crest and trough. He is my inspiration and has always helped me believe in each and every step of my career. Every life-changing decision we have made together, and Krish has encouraged me to believe in me, helping me to achieve my dream of becoming an award-winning chef. Now, the sky is the limit for this Mumbai girl!

Magical Mumbai Flavours

The Indian Way of Eating Meals

While teaching in schools in England, I was often asked by my students "Miss, do you eat with your fingers?" My answer was always, "Of course I do!" We all eat chips, sandwiches, finger food, pizza with our fingers, right? So why not daal with rice or curry with rice or curry with chapati?

Being born and brought up in Mumbai, I was lucky to experience multiregional cuisines and to experience other ways of life. I grew up eating "Thali food" – *Thali* is a Hindi word meaning 'a large plate'. It is now used as an expression for a type of eating in India - many different dishes served in small bowls arranged on a Thali or platter. As a family we always sat on the floor and enjoyed our evening meal together. Like many households in India, my everyday Thali always contained starters or finger food, main curries, rice, daal, chapati or pooris, papad, yoghurt and often a delicious dessert. I must admit, as a child I would have loved a dining table – you could already see how Western culture was influencing me. There is a reason for the sitting on the floor, though. According to Ayurveda (the alternative Indian medicine) sitting on the floor cross-legged like a yogi massages abdominal muscles and helps improve digestion.

In my childhood, eating with knife, fork and spoon was a novelty, but approaching traditional Thali with these implements would have been seen as sophisticated, although quite an awkward task. Eating with your fingers, like me in my childhood and my children now, is deemed unhygienic and nauseating, but according to Ayurveda and health experts, it is extremely healthy. My nan always used to say that eating your food with your fingers feeds not only the body but also the mind and soul. As a young girl, I never understood what she meant, but I always felt satisfied and happy. According to Ayurveda, each finger represents one of five elements (thumb for fire, forefinger for air, middle finger for space, ring finger for earth and the little finger for water). Whenever you touch food with your fingers to eat, the fingertips help your brain to connect with your food. By touching, you stimulate these five elements and invite *agni* (fire) to activate your digestive juices. By improving digestion, you become more conscious of tastes, textures and the aroma of the food you are eating, which enhances the pleasure of eating. In India and many countries like Sri Lanka, Nepal, Myanmar and parts of the Middle East, eating with fingers is perceived to be a sensual activity. The whole idea is that you should be able to enjoy the process of eating whilst using all your senses – taste, smell, sight and touch.*

A few days ago, I encouraged my children to eat their food with their fingers. Yes, we did have a messy table, but when I asked them what the food was like and how they felt about eating with fingers, my seven-year-old said the food tasted very nice. And my 14-year-old fussy eater said everything tasted truly scrumptious and finished all her food within minutes. If you have

* https://doctor.ndtv.com/living-healthy/are-there-any-health-benefits-of-sitting-on-the-floor-and-eating-ayurveda-tells-us-1828673
https://naturecareayurveda.com.au/yoga-and-eating-food-with-hands/
https://www.artofliving.org/in-en/lifestyle/best-way-to-eat-your-food

never tried it, try it today. Obviously, you will need utensils when eating pasta, lasagne, soup or a roast dinner, but do try it with Thai or African curries or risotto. It doesn't have to be Indian food to enjoy it this way. It's not difficult to use your fingers to eat, but there are certain rules which should be followed:

- In India we always eat with the right hand, as the left one is deemed unclean.

- Always use your fingertips and make sure the food doesn't touch your palm.

- It is important that you don't put your fingers in your mouth but push the food in with your thumb.

Techniques and Tips to Remember Before You Start with these Recipes

In my 28 years' experience of cooking, I only honestly say that traditional Indian cooking methods in India are not hugely different from those commonly used in other cuisines. There is a reason why Indian food is so flavoursome and aromatic: it's both the ingredients and spices you use and the cooking techniques you employ that make the dish a real show-stopper. The techniques and tips I am sharing in this book are the ones I grew up with as they were passed down through generations, with some extras of my own.

To make you feel more confident, if you have already used cooking methods like baking, boiling, sautéing, frying, then, believe me, you will absolutely fall in love with Indian cooking. Indians use all the above methods and more. The difference lies in how the techniques are applied during the cooking process.

Indian cooking is a simple art which is created with love, patience, some easy techniques, tips and a few ingredients. My nan, my best friend, always taught me that your attitude can easily affect your cooking and the food, so it is very important to cook everything with love, which is the most important ingredient. My advice to all the cooks and chefs in the world is to stay happy, and to bring those happy thoughts to enjoy the whole experience of cooking. Believe me, you will create not only magical dishes but also the best bond with your loved ones.

There are a few things which you have to consider and understand before you start with my recipes:

Use of mixer grinder or food processor or dry spice grinder

If you are a novice with Indian cooking, I would recommend the first thing to invest in is buying a mixer grinder or a food processor or a spice grinder. This makes your life much easier – from kneading dough to slicing, grating, grinding and blending. You can easily buy them online or from stores. I absolutely love my small spice grinder as well as mixer grinder as they help me to make the fine powder when I am grinding spices and making tomato purée or chutneys.

Pressure cooker

A pressure cooker not only is a time saver but also an energy saver (electricity and human!) and one of the most loved utensils in an Indian kitchen. In this book I have used a pressure cooker for a few recipes. It is very important to learn how to use a pressure cooker in Indian cooking. If you are cooking daal it takes 8–10 minutes to cook, whereas vegetables take 5 to 6 minutes, chicken curry dishes take 12–15 minutes and lamb curry dishes take 20–25 minutes. Personally, I like cooking meat on a slow heat in a *kadahi* (or heavy-bottomed pan) as I find slow-cooked meat tastes more delicious than pressure-cooked meat. Another benefit of using a pressure cooker or slow cooker is that the steaming helps retain the nutrients of vegetables and *daale* or lentils.

Tawa

Tawa is a concave, disc-shaped frying pan or griddle, usually made from cast iron or aluminium or carbon steel. There are easily available in Indian shops or online (www.amazon.com). Indians use tawa for chapatis, rotis, parathas and some more tawa dishes.

Start with a simple recipe if you are a learner or new to Indian cooking

The whole idea behind using this cookery book is for you to enjoy your cooking experience and make some magical and truly delicious dishes for you and your loved ones. Indian food has a bad reputation for being complex and spicy. And this is not true and unfair. Once you have familiarised yourself with spices, try to find easy recipes which have only a few instructions – i.e. masala chai (page 234) or mint and coriander chutney (page 228) – and give it a go.

Using knives

Knives play an important role when you are cooking Indian food. Please make sure that your knife is always sharp. You can either get them professionally sharpened or you can buy a knife sharpener from various websites and stores. I always recommend a chef's knife when you are chopping.

Read your recipe and be prepared

Please make sure that you always read your recipe from start to finish before you shop for ingredients and start cooking. I don't want you to be facing any surprise factors and getting frustrated.

Cooking Onions

Yes, crying over the chopping board again!

I am afraid you can't eliminate onions from Indian cooking as they play a very important role and form the basis of curry sauce. This versatile vegetable can either be cooked or used as a garnish. Most of the time onions either need to be chopped very fine or blended. From childhood, I have always seen my mum, my neighbours and my aunties cooking onions for different lengths of time for different types of dishes. For example, for daal you can either cook onions until they are golden, or you can boil onions with lentils, which happens very often at my in-laws.

Please always make sure that your oil is nice and hot before adding onions and then make sure that you spread the chopped onions so that they are exposed to the heat evenly. I always add ¼ tsp salt when I sauté onions as it quickens the process.

Quite a few recipes in this book begin with the instruction to heat the oil on a medium heat and cook the onions for 10–15 minutes until they are soft and translucent. There is a reason why they may need to be cooked for a longer duration.

When cooking vegetable curry I always cook onions for around 10–15 minutes until the onions are soft and light brown as it balances well with the dominant flavours of the other vegetables.

When cooking meat curries I always cook onions low and slow until they are a dark brown colour (approximately 20–25 minutes). The onions will become translucent first and then they start browning quickly. You must keep stirring your onions; if they are catching at the bottom just add a splash of water and stir. Cooking onions for longer will help make your tomato-based curry masala rich and dark.

Peeling garlic

Such hard work, isn't it? Peeling garlic is one tedious task which can take up quite some preparation time. The following are a few tricks I use in my home kitchen as well as in Dalvi's kitchen and I do hope that you find the following tricks helpful. Garlic is also essential in most Indian cooking. It has been proven by research that garlic used on a regular basis enhances immunity, reduces blood pressure, and plays a vital role in preventing cancer.*

- Remove cloves from the garlic bulb. Trim off the roots and place the clove under a large chef's knife, with the blade facing away from you.

* https://www.ncbi.nlm.nih.gov/pmc/articles/PMC5946235/
https://www.medicalnewstoday.com/articles/264599#1

Press down using the palm of your hand until you hear a crack. I use this method a lot when I am using only a few garlic cloves.

- When making garlic paste in a large quantity, I take garlic bulbs and remove the cloves, place the cloves in a mason jar and then screw on the cap. Then shake the jar for 20 seconds or so. Doing this means the skins break away easily.

- You can also use a microwave for peeling garlic. Take the garlic cloves from a bulb and put them in the microwave for about 20 seconds or so. Remove them from the microwave and let them cool down for 10 seconds or so. The skins will then come off easily.

Peeling ginger

When possible, I wash and use ginger with its skin because ginger is more nutritious with its skin. However, when making ginger paste at the restaurant, I use a spoon to peel off the ginger skin. I then make use of the removed ginger skin when making vegetable stock or my all-time favourite drink – my homemade ginger tea (see page 234). Here I am sharing my mum's technique of peeling ginger.

- Hold a piece of ginger root firmly in one hand and the bowl of a spoon firmly in the other hand and then scrape the edge of the spoon against the ginger to peel off the skin. I use this technique when I am making ginger paste. By doing this you don't take off a huge amount of ginger flesh with ginger skin. In case you find this difficult, just soak the piece of ginger in warm water for a few minutes to soften the skin.

- You can also use a vegetable peeler, but a peeler will scrape off a thicker layer, adding some wastage. But if the ginger is unruly and curved, then a peeler will remove the skin more conveniently.

- When chopping ginger, always use a sharp knife and slice it into coins. Slice the ginger across the grains of the fibres. This is because ginger is fibrous, and the fibres are always in the direction of the root of the ginger. So, if you chop in the same direction as the fibres, it will be more difficult to cut.

Sautéing or Bhuna

The Indian style of sautéing is called *bhuna*. Sautéing requires a very hot pan, then add a small amount of oil or ghee so that it is hot enough and then you add ingredients like onion, ginger, garlic and chillies to the pan on a medium heat until they have started softening. I always advise when doing cookery lessons, never crowd your pan so that the ingredients achieve the desired browning. If the pan is crowded, the food will steam or boil rather than sauté. Always remember to keep stirring so that the ingredients are cooked evenly. Once the above ingredients are cooked and have become brown, you add chopped tomatoes or tomato purée and cook until the raw smell of tomatoes disappears. And then you add spices, mix and add some water to prevent ingredients from sticking to the bottom of the pan. When the oil has separated (see the next point), you add meat or vegetables and stir until the meat pieces or vegetables are covered with this bhuna mixture.

Cook until the oil separates

In this recipe book, you will see instructions "cook until the oil separates". This is when you see bubbles appear and the oil making a thin layer on top of the gravy, sauce or curry (without any vegetable or meat or fish pieces). This stage shows that all the masalas (spices powder) have been cooked properly and the right balance of base flavour has been reached. It takes 10 to 12 minutes. This process needs a little patience. Please don't be tempted to turn the heat to maximum, because that will burn the masala mixture.

Add water gradually

When cooking vegetable curry or meat curry, always remember to add stock or hot water gradually in stages. Otherwise, there will be too much liquid and you will spend a lot of time boiling that off, which will affect the flavours and nutrition of your curry.

Remember to put the lid on

Always remember to put the lid on when cooking any curry dishes as it quickens the cooking process using built-up steam.

Remember to taste

If you are cooking curries, always taste before you serve so that you can add and adjust salt, chilli powder, garam masala and coriander powder. When it comes to vegetable starters, i.e. pakoras or samosa or tikkies, I always taste them before I deep or shallow fry. When it comes to meat pakoras or tikkas, I cook just one first, taste and then adjust the spices and salt if needed. Please note that salt plays an important role when tasting as it balances all the spices and brings out the best in your spices.

Be organised and stay tidy

Please make sure that the kitchen work surface is clean. Always have the ingredients, pots and pans ready before you cook. Please don't forget to pull out all of the required spices from your cupboard; otherwise, you will waste time finding a needed spice and that will ultimately affect your dish. I want you to enjoy the whole cooking experience and create super-delicious dishes for you and your loved ones!

Tempering (*Tadka* or *Chhonk* or *Baghaar*)

Tadka is a technique that uses infused oil, which adds an extra layer of flavour and gives that special aroma. Although many chefs say the oil needs to be smoking hot for *tadka* to work, for me it doesn't work because there is a real chance that the spice seeds like cumin seeds, mustard seeds and other aromatics like garlic or ginger, dry chillies and curry leaves will burn and lose the desired aroma and fail to make your dish tasty. I always suggest making sure that oil is warm over a high heat and then advise adding spice seeds, garlic, ginger, dry chillies and curry leaves on a medium heat, as in this way you have more control over spices and their aromas.

Deep frying or *Talna*

There are a few recipes in this book which need deep frying or shallow frying. For deep frying, you can either use the *kadahi* or a heavy wok-shaped pan. Always make sure that your wok or *kadahi* is completely dry before you add oil. I always recommend filling your wok or *kadahi* with oil until you have reached slightly more than half of the pan.

Heat oil on a high heat until it reaches 160°C to 180°C. The best way to check is either to take a small piece of bread, a batter you use for frying or one small piece of onion, and drop this into the oil. If that piece comes up straight away, that means you are all ready to fry. (You can always use a temperature probe.)

I usually turn the hob down to medium to high heat before I start deep frying so that pakoras or samosas are fried evenly and look fresh instead of becoming dark brown very quickly but not being cooked on the inside.

Please do not overcrowd your pan and always remember to fry in batches. Always use a slotted spatula or spoon when removing fried food from the oil.

Place fried food on a plate or a tray lined with paper towels to drain.

Once you have finished deep frying, let the oil cool down completely. Strain the oil into an airtight container. You will be able to reuse this oil for cooking.

Removing turmeric stains

Turmeric is the most used spice in Indian cooking. So, you are bound to get that yellow stain on your clothes at one time or another! If you get a yellow stain on your kitchen work surface, you can easily get rid of it by cleaning with a bleach spray or detergent or using a paste made of baking soda and water. Apply this paste to stained areas and leave for 10 minutes or so, then scrub and wipe clean.

If you have spilt some turmeric on your clothes or tea towels, you must act fast and treat that stain before it has a chance to dry out. The best thing to do is to dab the stain with cold water and laundry detergent. If your clothes or tea towels can tolerate bleach, soak in mild bleach solution as it's the best way to get the stain out. After soaking, wash the stained clothes immediately either in the washing machine or by hand-washing.

If you get turmeric stains on your dishes or blender or food processor jars, you can use bleach or vinegar. Use a 2:1 ratio of water and bleach. I usually fill my sink with that ratio and soak my jars in this liquid for 10 minutes or so.

More Than Just Ingredients

Since my childhood, I have never seen my mum, nan, friends' mums, neighbours and aunties use measuring scales when cooking. And that's exactly the habit I have got into. Whether I am home or at the restaurant, I never use any measurements when cooking Indian curries, snacks, soups and bread. And this will come to you too once you start cooking Indian food on a regular basis. You must understand the spices you use in your cooking. Even though there is a lot of information available in the internet world, I am sharing my knowledge of spices and I am sure you will find this chapter helpful.

You can find and buy all or most of the ingredients mentioned in this cookery book either from Indian grocery shops around your area or places like Red Rickshaw, Taj Spices or even Amazon.

Understanding herbs and spices

Herbs and Spices have been used for years in Indian cooking because of their medicinal benefits. They are the heart and soul of Indian cooking and are a natural way to add flavours and aromas to your dish. It is vital that you understand herbs and spices as they bring that unique aroma to your dishes.

While there are no particular rules on the order of adding spices while cooking, it all depends on the recipe you are following and the type of dish you are cooking. You must understand when to add which spice to ensure you get the flavour that makes Indian food unique. Like many Indian households, I add ground spices like turmeric, garam masala, coriander powder and chilli powder when the cooking process is halfway along. I always add fresh coriander, mint leaves and dry fenugreek leaves or *kasuri methi* at the end when the cooking process is finished because the flavours of these herbs are delicate.

One thing you must remember is that less is more when it comes to Indian cooking. Adding too many spices or too much of one spice can make a dish bitter. The use of spices depends on what dish you are cooking. For example, when I am cooking a simple vegetable curry, I don't add too many spices to balance out the flavour and taste of the vegetables. On the other hand, when I am cooking a meat curry, I add extra chilli powder or extra garam masala or cardamom powder to enhance the taste of that curry.

Always remember to store your whole spices in an airtight container away from direct sunlight, heat and moisture. You don't have to keep them in a refrigerator.

Usually, spice powders will lose their potency after six to eight months, so if you use shop-brought garam masala and use it up within that time that's fine. Otherwise, I always recommend buying whole spices as they can last up to a year and make a small batch of freshly garam masala and coriander powder in advance.

1) *Hing* (Asafoetida)

Hing, also known as asafoetida or sometimes 'devil's dung', is an essential spice in Indian cooking that can transform your dish into something magical. *Hing* has a strong pungent smell and is a gum from a variety of giant fennel. While it's native to Afghanistan and Iraq, it is commonly used in most Indian households. As in many households, my mum used to put small pieces of asafoetida rocks in containers of lentils, rice and spices, as the strong odour always kept bugs and insects away. The yellow powdered asafoetida is always used in cooking. Yes, it does have a strong odour but when it is cooked, its smell becomes more palatable, similar to garlic.

I remember drinking *hing* water as a child when I had an upset tummy and feeling better in 20 to 30 minutes. According to *Ayurveda*, asafoetida is very good for digestion and any gastric problems. When I am cooking for a family of four, I use just a pinch of asafoetida as that's enough to give the aroma and to help digestion.*

2) Cumin seeds or *Jeera*

Cumin is a staple ingredient not only in Indian cooking but also in Mexican and North African cooking. In this book, you will be using brown cumin seeds and ground cumin seeds. They are easily available in supermarkets or online. Cumin is a spice that belongs to the same family as fennel. Cumin doesn't only enhance the flavours of your dishes but also helps to digest food and improves iron levels. It is also known as a metabolic stimulant. To improve my metabolism, one of my morning rituals is to boil three cups of water, then add ½ tsp cumin seeds, ¼ tsp fenugreek seeds and ½ tsp black onion seeds when the water is boiling. Put the lid back on and let it boil for another 2 minutes.

---

* https://www.sciencedirect.com/topics/agricultural-and-biological-sciences/asafoetida
https://www.easyayurveda.com/2013/02/12/asafoetida-health-benefits-medicinal-uses-ayurveda/
https://academic.oup.com/fqs/article/2/1/1/4823052

Magical Mumbai Flavours

Then turn the heat off and when the water is lukewarm, mix ½ tsp organic honey and drink.

3) Carom seeds or *Ajwain*

Carom seeds – *Ajwain* in Hindi and *Ugragandha* in Sanskrit – is a spice that goes hand in hand when cooking samosas, onion bhajis, pakoras, parathas and pickles. Without carom seeds, these dishes are just incomplete.

Ajwain is derived from a herb found in India. It is smaller than a cumin seed in size and varies from slightly olive green to brown in colour. The seeds have a bit spicy and pungent flavour and smell similar to oregano.

From my own experience, I can definitely say that the health benefits it has are just unbelievable. It helps immensely to maintain digestive health. If you are struggling with any tummy aches due to indigestion or a burning sensation, take ¼ tsp carom seeds with warm water. Thank you to my nan for sharing this medicinal trick with me, as this always has and is still doing magic in the Dalvi household. (On a funny note, you will be amazed at the amount of wind you can pass!)

Ajwain also helps treat the common cold. For instance, when my children struggle with colds and suffer with a blocked nose, I always roast carom seeds slightly, tie them in a thin cloth, encourage the children to inhale this cloth frequently and keep it near to their pillow so that they can inhale as they sleep. If you live outside India, carom seeds are easily available in Indian shops or herbal shops or online.

4) Fennel seeds or *Sauf*

This is another popular ingredient which you will find in most Indian households. This green seed has a crunchy texture on the outside with a mildly sweet flavour. As a child, I never liked it when it was in my curry or in pilau but always loved it as a mouth freshener after eating my meals. Indians are food lovers and most of them consume fennel seeds after their meal for faster digestion. As per *Ayurveda*, the essential oil of the fennel seeds not only stimulates the secretion of digestive juices but also possesses antibacterial properties that help to freshen your breath. And that's why when you get your bill in Indian restaurants, most of the time the waiting staff bring a small bowl of fennel seeds too.*

---

* https://www.planetayurveda.com/library/fennel-foeniculum-vulgare-uses-health-benefits/

5) Coriander seeds and fresh coriander leaves

In Indian culinary drama, coriander (*koris* in Greek) has its own written character and is irreplaceable. Coriander always makes an entrance, whether it's a grand solo or as a supporting cast. Indian food is not complete without this spice and/or herb. It finds its way into almost all Indian dishes, whether in the form of leaves for garnishing, stalks in soup, seeds in starters or curries, or in powder form.

Some people do not approve of coriander in their meals; to them, it tastes soapy. The soapiness in coriander is created by a compound known as *aldehydes*, which is also found in soap too. Some have tastebuds that are very reactive to a*ldehydes*, so when indulging dishes garnished with coriander leaves they are particularly reminded of soap. What is interesting, however, is that when coriander leaves are blended with other herbs and spices, the evolving chemistry breaks down *aldehydes* and all of a sudden, the food lovers who did not approve of coriander leaves as a garnish enjoy their dishes with coriander in a hidden form. Fascinating, isn't it?*

Coriander seeds are popularly known as *Dhana* or *dhania dana* in India. Like cumin seeds, they are extensively used across many households in India to flavour curries, snacks, breakfast, rice dishes and masala. This spice is not only popular in Indian cooking but is also one of the main ingredients in Mexican cuisine, where it is utilised in salsas and meat dishes. Coriander seeds are green or brown; they are plump and have a hollow cavity which carries essential oil.

6) Fenugreek seeds or *Methi Dana*

Many households in India use this important ingredient in their cooking and for beauty and hair. I remember my mum covering my hair with *mehndi* or henna with fenugreek seed paste or sometimes powder not only for colouring purposes but for naturally conditioning too. These small chocolate colour seeds are packed with nutrients which are essential for the body. My dad, who has diabetes, has been drinking fenugreek seed water every morning and he sees the benefit as it helps to reduce blood sugar. According to *Ayurveda*, *methi* water helps weight loss and is good for the liver, kidneys and metabolism. I have used fenugreek seeds in dishes like Malvani chicken or Kerala-style lamb (see page 137). But if you want to add a few *methi dana* to every dish, that won't do any harm.**

* See: https://www.sciencefocus.com/the-human-body/why-does-coriander-taste-like-soap-to-some-people/

** https://maharishiayurvedaindia.com/blogs/ayurveda-knowledge-center/amazing-benefits-of-fenugreek

7) Turmeric or *Haldi*

For most of my dishes, I use turmeric (*Haldi* in Hindi). It comes from the root of *Curcuma longa*, a leafy plant related to ginger. It is usually boiled, sun-dried and then ground into a powder. *Haldi* has a bright yellow colour and a pungent, warm, earthy aroma and taste. Although it can be bitter if used in excessive amounts. It is a key ingredient in Indian cooking and can be used as a natural colouring agent.

Haldi is my favourite spice not only because it gives a fantastic colour and flavours to food but also because it has medicinal properties. I remember my mother giving me a warm cup of milk mixed with half a teaspoon of turmeric, a quarter teaspoon of ground peppercorn and a teaspoon of honey when I used to have a bad cold and cough. I never used to like the taste but that drink always did its magic and still does. Believe it or not, I still follow that tradition when my children or husband have coughs and colds. I also remember the days when my mother used to put turmeric powder on my wounds or cuts whenever I got hurt, because it is a natural antiseptic used for healing cuts and wounds. As a child, I always thought it was a magic medicine! A study in September 2014 found that the curcumin in turmeric offers some beneficial properties that accelerate the wound healing process by soothing irritation and oxidation.*

8) Black peppercorns or *kaali Mirchi*

Black pepper is one of the most widely traded spices in the world. As we all know, it appears in more or less every cuisine. It is used not only as spice but also as medicine. The presence of piperine, a bioactive, gives peppercorns their biting and pungent spiciness and woody aroma. For the recipes in this book, I have used roasted black peppercorns for masalas (see page 204) and ground black pepper in a few recipes.

For me, turmeric and black pepper are the best of friends. They work together really well. As research says, curcumin in turmeric has antioxidant, antiseptic, antifungal and anti-inflammatory properties, while black pepper has properties that improve digestion and boosts metabolism. Greger (2015) says that the curcumin in turmeric is poorly absorbed into the bloodstream. It cannot be used properly by our bodies because of its poor bioavailability. As a result, you could be missing out on its advantages to health. This is where black pepper plays an important role, as it has an extremely healthy bioactive component. This piperine in black pepper when combined with the curcumin in turmeric enhances curcumin absorption by up to 2000% (Goodson, 2018).

* https://journals.cambridgemedia.com.au/wpr/volume-25-number-3/evidence-summary-turmeric-curcumin-wound-management-limited-resources-communities-lrcs

In addition to helping with absorption, studies have also found that piperine improves the bioactivity of curcumin in human bodies. The best part is that there are no side effects from consuming turmeric and black pepper together. I told you that they are the best of friends, didn't I?!*

9) Cloves or *Laung*
I use cloves in my curries because they have a warming, spicy and sweet taste. Most of us have used cloves or clove oil when suffering with toothache. According to research, cloves are actually good sources of vitamin C, calcium and Omega 3 fatty acids. My mother-in-law always says that cloves help digestive and stomach disorders but for me, I use them for the aroma they bring to my dishes.

10) Small Black Mustard seeds or *Raee*
These strong-flavoured mustard seeds are mostly added for tempering. They are very popular in South-Indian, Maharashtrian, Gujrati and Bengali cooking. I just love an appetizing aroma of mustard seeds when I am tempering for daal or upma (see page 181) or any south Indian dishes.

11) Raw mango powder or *Amchur*
Amchur is dried raw mango powder and is widely used in Indian cooking. Its sweet and sour flavour is truly mouth-watering and it's a must-have ingredient in your kitchen cupboard. If you live outside India, amchur is easily available in Indian shops or online (www.amazon.com).

12) Cardamoms or *Elaichi*
Cardamom has a strong and complex yet inviting aroma and has a 'piney' and almost menthol-like flavour. Cardamom is widely used in Indian and Middle Eastern cuisine. There are two kinds of cardamom: black and green. I use whole black cardamom for cooking curries or rice dishes or making dry masalas and green cardamom, either whole or ground, when making Indian dessert or pudding. Please note, choosing one over the other will really alter the overall taste. Always remember to pick out black cardamom pods after cooking, as biting into them will taste unpleasant!

* https://www.bbc.co.uk/programmes/articles/PSTGKKt3HRo8tmK69w7J1b/does-turmeric-really-help-protect-us-from-cancer https://timesofindia.indiatimes.com/life-style/food-news/what-happens-when-you-mix-black-pepper-and-turmeric/articleshow/70977129.cms

13) Saffron or *Kesar*

The most expensive spice. Have you ever wondered why this spice is so expensive? Saffron is obtained from saffron crocus, a flower that has lilac-coloured petals. There are always three strands in the flower. These strands can only be removed from the plant by hand. According to research, it takes around 112,500 strands to make up half a pound of saffron spice. As I mentioned before, there are only three strands or stigmas in each flower: this means that around 37,500 flowers are used to make that small quantity. Once these strands are handpicked, they are carefully laid on a sieve and cured over heat to amplify the flavour.

Although saffron has a very strong flavour, I mainly use it for its health benefits and colour properties. I find it mind-blowing how just a pinch gives so much colour – and yes, it smells amazing too!

In my childhood, my mum used to give all of us what she used to call "magic milk". It had honey, ground nuts and saffron in it. She always used to say that almonds with saffron boost your memory. Believe it or not, that was my favourite drink of the day. Research shows that several active components of saffron may boost the memory and improve learning skills.*

14) Bay Leaves or *Tejpatta*

The bay leaves we get in the United Kingdom are very different from Indian bay leaves (*tejpatta*). These are long, wide, and pale green in colour, whereas the bay leaves we get in the UK supermarkets are small and have a slightly darker green colour. The aroma is very different too. When I am buying bay leaves, I always smell them first and if they smell like a cinnamon stick that's a true *tejpatta* for me. You can easily find Indian bay leaves either in Indian stores or online. Or you can substitute the bay leaves you get in the UK.

15) Cinnamon sticks or *Dalchini*

Cinnamon sticks or *dalchini* come from the bark of a tree. The spice is very popular in Indian cooking. It has a sweet taste and an exotic fragrance. It has anti-inflammatory properties to reduce stomach disorders. It is used in curry dishes as well as desserts and drinks. Please don't go crazy when using this for cooking: an inch of cinnamon stick is enough if you are cooking curry for four to five people. Please note: a good quality cinnamon stick always has a strong and pleasant smell.

* https://www.healthline.com/nutrition/saffron
https://recipes.howstuffworks.com/food-facts/saffron.htm

16) Black onion (Nigella) seeds or *Kalonji*

I'm not sure why these seeds are called black onion seeds: I seriously don't think there is any connection between *kalonji* and onion. But never mind, I like this ingredient because these seeds not only give an amazing flavour to your food but have an absolutely wonderful visual effect as they stand out prominently when you take photos. *Kalonji* or nigella seeds come from the fruit of a flower called *Nigella sativa*. In India, roasted nigella seeds are used for flavouring daal, naans, pickles, samosas and some curries. These seeds have a distinct aroma and taste similar to cumin seeds and oregano.

17) Star Anise

Star anise is predominately used in Chinese cooking but is also used in Indian cooking. I use this flower when I am cooking biryani or garam masala.

18) Mace flower or *Javitiri*

Mace is a yellow-brown, lace-like spice and comes from the protective coating of a nutmeg kernel. Mace's flavour and aroma differ slightly from nutmeg: its taste is milder. It is used in recipes which are delicately flavoured. I use mace when cooking biryani and spice blends.

19) Chillies or *Mirchi*

When cooking I use either green chillies, whole red chillies, chilli powder or sometimes a combination of all of them. Believe it or not, Indian cooking didn't use chillies until the 15th century. They were brought to India by the Portuguese towards the end of the 15th century. And now India is one of the world's largest chilli producers.

I always use either whole Kashmiri red chillies (or powder) as they are less spicy and give a lovely colour to curries, or I use bydegi chillies (or powder) for meat curries as they are spicier. When it comes to green chillies, the general rule of thumb is that the smaller and darker the colour of the chilli, the spicier the food will get. I am sure you will find this information helpful when selecting and following recipes from this book!

20) Black salt or *Kala Namak*

Me : *Nani, yain chaat main swad nahi hai, kya karu?* (This chaat does not taste nice, what should I do?)
Nan : *thoda sa kala namak daal dey!* (Add some black salt powder to it!)

My nan's mantra was to add black salt powder to make any finger food, fruit salad or chaat dishes super-delicious. Her chaats were particularly famous in her village. Indian black salt (*kala namak*) is Indian volcanic rock salt. It contains trace impurities of sulphates, iron and magnesium which all contribute to the salt's colour, taste and rotten egg smell. Despite its name, black salt is a pinkish colour when ground. It has a pungent, savoury and umami flavour and is commonly used in Indian cooking. It adds a distinctive flavour to dishes and is known to be a healthy form of salt.

21) Curry leaves or *Kadipatta*

Kadipatta or sweet neem leaves are very popular in Southern, West Coast Indian and Sri Lankan cooking. They are usually fried along with cumin seeds and mustard seeds in the first stage of cooking when you are cooking dishes like upma (page 181), Red snapper curry (page 153) and Kerala-style lamb curry (page 137). These leaves have a short shelf life, and they can't be kept in the fridge for long. When using at home, I usually wash these leaves, dry the with kitchen towel and then freeze them very loosely packed in an airtight container for a few weeks. You can also buy the dry *kaddipatta* – and yes, their shelf life is better when compared with fresh leaves. I don't like using dry sweet neem leaves as I don't like compromising on the aroma that fresh *kaddipatta* brings.

22) Gram flour or *Besan*

Besan or gram flour is made of channa daal or Bengal gram. *Besan* is used in many Indian households, either for cooking purposes or for beauty. *Besan* or gram flour is easily available in supermarkets or online. *Besan* is used for pakoras, parathas and sometimes in curries like Dhaba Chicken (page 121) too.

23) Coconut

Coconut is an essential ingredient for South Indian and Maharashtrian cooking such as Malvani chicken (page 131) and Kerala Lamb (page 137). It is used in many forms – raw, as oil, as milk, dry or *khopbra*, or desiccated. You can easily find coconut chunks, coconut milk, desiccated coconut and coconut oil in supermarkets. For the recipes I have shared in this book, you will need desiccated coconut, coconut oil and coconut milk.

24) Nuts

Nuts are very important in Indian cooking, whether cooking curry dishes such as biryani or Indian desserts. Most of the nuts used in this recipe book are cashews, almonds or pistachios.

25) Chapati flour or *atta*

Chapati atta is made of wholewheat. Every household in India has chapatis. Nowadays there are various kinds of chapati flours, but I always use pure wholewheat flour. This is easily available in supermarkets or Indian grocery shops near you, or you can order online.

26) Semolina or *Rava* or *Sooji*

Semolina is a coarse flour that is made from durum wheat and can vary from yellow to off-white in colour. Semolina can have a more earthy aroma than regular wheat flour. It is a high-gluten, high-protein flour.

27) All-purpose flour or *Maida*

This is another important ingredient which every Indian household has. All-purpose flour, also known as refined flour, is made from wheat grains after removing the brown kernel. It is then milled, refined and bleached. Maida is white and powdery and is used for many recipes like naan (page 189), ouzi (page 163), samosas (page 59) and slurry.

28) Nylon sev

Nylon sev is a popular and thin noodle-like snack made from gram flour paste, which is seasoned with turmeric powder and salt before being fried in oil. They are used as decoration on chaat or bhel puri or on upma.

29) Jaggery or *Gud or Gur*

Jaggery always takes me back to my playful childhood days when with my brother and sister I used to eat hot chapati cooked by my nan with homemade ghee and *gur*. The flavour of jaggery is just heavenly (as I am typing my mouth is drooling). Jaggery is unrefined sugar made from raw and concentrated sugar cane juice. Jaggery is used mainly for Indian desserts or pudding or tea or chutneys. It is less sweet and healthier than refined sugar. Jaggery can vary in colour from pale yellow to dark brown and can be bought either in block form or as a powder.

30) Kokum

Kokum, also known as the *Garcinia indica* plant, is native to the Western Ghat region of India – the Gujrat and Konkan regions. It's a small fruit which is red in colour and deepens to purple on ripening. The dried variety of kokum is used in cooking. It has a sour taste with a bit of a sweet aroma. It is popular due to its taste and medicinal qualities. It has been known as 'Grandma's cure' and is said to aid digestion and acidity.

31) Tamarind

Tamarind is used in prune, date and tamarind chutney in this book (see page 232). Tamarind is sold as a block, a paste and a concentrate. But for making prune, date and tamarind chutney (page 232) I have used a block. Tamarind is used in curries or chutneys to add a touch of sourness.

32) Rose water

You might be thinking… floral taste with food…. yes, if a tiny drop of rose water is used the right way, believe me, you will love this ingredient. Rose water is not only used in Indian cuisine but is also popular in Mediterranean and Middle Eastern cuisines. Rose water is a by-product of making rose perfume, an ancient process that originated in Persia. You will need rose water for making Lamb biryani (page 158) and the dessert Shahi tukda (page 223).

33) Lentils or *Daale*

Daal is the most versatile staple food in every Indian household. Whether it is *tuar* (split pigeon peas or *arhar daal*) or *masoor daal* (red split lentils) or *channa daal* or *urad*, *daal* is an integral part of the Indian family. Lentils are healthy, flavourful and full of nutrients and taste.

34) Ginger or *Adrak*

A very popular spice used in Indian and Chinese cooking. The flavour of ginger is peppery and slightly sweet, while the aroma is spicy and pungent. In this book, I have used either fresh ginger or ginger powder in almost every recipe! Ginger has been used in food and for medicinal purposes for a long time. I absolutely love ginger just because it gives off a fantastic aroma as well as being so good for your body and health. I must have my ginger tea (page 234) every morning – I am not talking about ginger-flavoured tea you get in supermarkets, but I am talking about tea made with fresh ginger. My nan, my mum and my mother-in-law always believed that ginger not only helps in digestion but also keeps illnesses like colds, coughs and sore throats away from your doorstep. Recent research has shown that the anti-inflammatory components in ginger can shorten the discomfort of headaches, colds and flu. According to *Ayurveda*, raw ginger benefits the joints as it helps to reduce joint swelling in people who suffer from arthritis. Ginger helps break down the accumulation of toxins in the organs. It can help promote healthy sweating, which can assist in detoxification during colds and flu.*

35) Garlic or *Lehsun*

Lots of it, please! Indian cooking is not complete without garlic. Garlic is a member of the onion family and has a spicy and pungent flavour. Please don't consume it raw, as the taste can be very strong and harsh. I'm not sure whether this is true, but it is said that the ancient Egyptians gave garlic to the slaves constructing the pyramids in order to increase their efficiency and stamina! According to researchers at the Garlic Research Bureau in Suffolk, England, even small amounts of garlic will have a pronounced effect on the breaking down of blood clots. Their studies also suggest that garlic may lower the risk of colon cancer by 35 per cent and stomach cancer by as much as 50 per cent.

Ginger and garlic not only add incredible flavour and aroma to many kinds of dishes, but they are also the real health boosters. While ginger and garlic are available in dried powder and supplement form, I personally feel that they are more effective in fresh form and they do rule in my kitchen.**

36) Mint or *Pudina*

Mint, that well-known mouth freshener, is a herb with remarkable medicinal properties. We see lots of mint products like chewing gum, mouthwash, toothpaste, etc. Most of us are only familiar with its refreshing aspect, but it has much more to offer than that. Mint leaves play a vital role in promoting digestion, reducing inflammation and soothing the stomach. According to *Ayurveda*, mint has an aroma which activates the saliva glands in our mouth as well as glands which secrete digestive enzymes, thereby facilitating digestion. Thus, it is extensively used in Indian cuisine. It can also enhance appetite and help ease nausea.***

---

* https://mapi.com/blogs/articles/ginger-an-ayurvedic-medicine-chest

** https://www.betternutrition.com/conditions-and-wellness/immunity-tips/medicinal-foods-garlic-ginger/

***https://maharishiayurvedaindia.com/blogs/ayurveda-knowledge-center/benefits-of-peppermint

37) Yoghurt

For most of the recipes mentioned in this book, I have used full-fat thick Greek yoghurt or natural yoghurt, as they have a creamier texture. To avoid curdling, I always whisk lightly before I marinade meat or mix it into the curry. If you are not a fan of yoghurt you can use coconut milk or coconut yoghurt.

38) Cooking oil

For most Indian cooking, the best oils to use are sunflower, vegetable and mustard oil. My personal favourite is sunflower as it's light and not as sticky and smelly compared to the other two. You will notice that I haven't used ghee (clarified butter) for many recipes. Finding a good quality ghee in the UK is difficult, and the really good ones are expensive to buy. Where I have had to use ghee in these recipes, I have used organic ghee. Sunflower oil and vegetable oil are easily available and because they are flavourless, they are ideal for Indian cooking.

39) Salt or *Namak*

Salt is essential in cooking as it always helps to bring out the flavours in your food. Your dish should be flavoursome and not salty. So, getting that balance right is very important. When you are roasting your whole spices, always make sure that you add a bit of salt as it helps brings flavours out of whole spices, binds all the ingredients together really well and works as a natural preservative to increase shelf life.

What to do if you have added too much salt – yes, we all have done that so many times! Okay, try the following tricks to remove the excess salt in curries.

- Add a small ball of chapati dough to the sauce or gravy and let it sit for 10 minutes or so and then remove it. This dough ball will absorb the excess salt.

- Squeeze half a lemon in the gravy or curry sauce.

- Or you can add mashed potato.

40) Tomatoes or *Tamatar*

Like onions, ginger and garlic fresh tomatoes play an important role in Indian cooking. They not only give that tangy flavour but also a red colour and thickness to your curry. I always like using fresh tomatoes but if you are in rush, you can use store-bought tomato purée too.

41) Spinach and spinach purée

When I am cooking, I always add washed spinach leaves a minute before I turn off the hob in order to preserve the nutritional value of the leaves. When making spinach purée, to keep the green colour and nutrition of spinach I cook it the following way: For 200 g of spinach, boil 2 cups of water. When the water is boiling, add spinach leaves and turn off the hob. Stir the spinach for a minute or so and then transfer the leaves to icy cold water for 20 to 30 seconds and blend it to a smooth purée with a pinch of salt.

Understanding the Diversity of Culinary Heritage

As you know, India is a massive country and very diverse when it comes to culinary traditions. Indian cuisine is divided into a few basic regional cuisines – North Indian, Central Indian, East Indian, South Indian and West Indian. And every region is unique in their own way of cooking and presentation of food. For example, when I cook Kerala lamb (page 137) I start with coconut oil and then add curry leaves, mustard seeds, cumin seeds, whereas when I cook malwani chicken from Maharashtra (page 131) I make a coconut and onion based mix called *"watap"* or *"watan"*; when I cook any Bengali dish I start with mustard oil and add mustard seeds, cumin seeds, fennel seeds and sometimes nigella seeds. So now you can see the relationship between the land/coast and its richness in natural resources and the inseparable relation among various recipes derived from this richness.

It is very important to understand this culinary heritage and what spices bring what flavours.

Is Indian Food Authentic?

The history of the evolution of Indian cuisine is just fascinating.* For the last several centuries, Indian food has constantly adopted new ingredients into its cuisine. From the Vedic civilisation which defined better form of cultivation, to Maurya culture which taught us all about basic kitchen manners, to the Gupta empire, which was influenced by Buddhism and Jainism, prohibiting the consumption of meat of animals (for they were considered sacred in a few religions), to Mughal cuisine, to the Portuguese, and then to the British Raj. Mughal cuisine brought inspirational and innovative skills that remain highly influential in Indian culinary practice. The Mughals introduced dishes like biryani and samosa which are widely popular not only in India but also throughout the whole world. During this Mughal invasion, breads such as tandoori roti, roomali roti and naan were also gifted to Indian cuisine; these are still cooked and enjoyed in many Indian household as well as restaurants. After the Mughals, India witnessed the arrival of the Portuguese who introduced dishes like vindaloo, sweet Goan wine and pav or *pau*. They introduced many vegetables and fruits like potatoes, tomatoes, papaya, guava, peanuts, pineapples and, let's not forget, chillies. *Yes, you read that right*! Indians always used spices in their food but not chillies before the Portuguese made their appearance in India. There is, of course, a strong Portuguese influence in Goan cuisine.** And then there was the entry of the British Empire (starting out as the East India Company), which ruled India for 200 years and introduced the cultivation of tea to Indian soil. They also introduced vegetables like cauliflowers, cabbages, carrots and spinach.

Many common ingredients used in Indian cooking are not actually native to India. Hence, I would like to say the authenticity of the Indian culinary heritage has always been evolving and creative, and that's why I don't think there is such a thing as 'authentic' Indian food.

---

* https://www.bbc.com/travel/article/20190609-the-surprising-truth-about-indian-food
https://indianculture.gov.in/food-and-culture/evolution-indian-gastronomy/evolution-indian-gastronomy-tale-fusion
https://journalofethnicfoods.biomedcentral.com/articles/10.1186/s42779-022-00129-4
https://www.trendmantra.com/the-evolution-of-indian-food/

** https://www.hindustantimes.com/brunch/the-portuguese-contribution-that-usually-goes-unheralded/story-sHINlLSQx7kZYjFFDhob3H.html

Street Food from Mumbai

Mumbai – a city that never sleeps and one that is known for its many lip-smacking dishes.

Mumbai is a financial and mercantile capital hub attracting people from every state and every background in India to follow their dreams. It's a dream land for many and a land of realisation, from richest to poorest, a city which looks after everyone.

When you are in Mumbai, street food becomes an inseparable part of your life. Take a stroll through Mumbai streets, and you are bound to discover limitless choices when it comes to innovative and delicious foods to try. Street food was a major part of my life. I still remember buying vada pav and samosas from my school canteen, standing outside the university around the *sandwich-wala* (Wala is a suffix for vendors or hawkers or mobile food carts – for example, *chai wala*, *samosa wala*, *fruit juice wala*, *paper wala*) and enjoying a toasted sandwich with my friends, going out with my work colleagues for quick lunch bites and an energetic cup of *masala chai*. In my day, street food carts were a meeting point and the source of countless memories and unforgettable, loud laughter.

In this street food section, I endeavour to present selective yet popular street food delicacies. I do hope that you will enjoy these recipes and that they will help you create your own memories with your loved ones.

- *Vada (or Wada) Pav*
- *Anda Bhurji Pav*
- *Mumbai Cheese Masala Toast Sandwich*
- *Pav Bhaji*
- *Vegetable Schezwan or Sichuan Noodles*

Vada (or Wada) Pav

If you take a walk down any street or alley or *Galli* of Mumbai, you can never miss the almighty vada pav: a dish which does not discriminate and gives you immense pleasure. It is a budget-friendly burger that hails from the streets of Mumbai. In my school days, the only motivation to attend school on Mondays was the mighty vada pav and enjoy an opportunity to miss homemade food over this street food.

Vada pav was invented by Ashok Vaidya, who used to sell them outside Dadar railway station.* Ashok's creation of vada pav was especially targeted toward mill-workers. They came across all over India, but the majority were from the state of Maharashtra. For these mill-workers, who left their families behind so that they could build an empire for their loved ones, but then forgot to look after themselves, the almighty vada pav was the saviour; so was the pav bhaji. I have discussed this later in this book (page 49).

Vada pav is a classic example of cultural fusion and union. It is a marriage of the Maharashtrian-style cooked *batata* (potato) vada (patty) and the Portuguese origin pav (bread rolls), the perfect union spruced up with lip-smackingly sweet, tangy and spicy chutney.

Ingredients (2 people – makes 4 vadas)

(For potato patty)

2 large white potatoes, boiled and coarsely mashed

2 tbsp cooking oil (preferably sunflower oil)

¼ tsp mustard seeds

¼ tsp cumin seeds

1 tbsp crushed curry leaves (preferably fresh)

½ inch of ginger, peeled and finely chopped

2 garlic cloves, peeled and finely chopped

1 to 4 green chillies (according to taste)

¼ tsp turmeric powder

Salt to taste

1 tbsp chopped coriander leaves

(For vada batter)

1 cup or 125 g gram flour (Besan)

Salt (to taste)

¼ tsp turmeric

Some water

Oil for deep frying

* https://timesofindia.indiatimes.com/life-style/food-news/vada-pav-history-of-the-popular-mumbai-snack/articleshow/76973714.cms

Instructions

1) Heat 2 tbsp oil in a pan on a medium heat.

2) When the oil is hot, add cumin seeds and mustard seeds.

3) When the seeds start releasing aromas, add curry leaves, finely chopped garlic, ginger and green chillies and sauté for a minute on a medium heat.

4) Now add turmeric powder and sauté for 30 seconds.

5) Add mashed potatoes, salt, and finely chopped coriander leaves. Mix everything well. Put the lid on and cook on a low heat for 2 minutes.

6) Turn off the heat. Let the mixture cool down before you start making small balls.

7) Meanwhile, get the gram flour batter ready. Take a bowl, add gram flour, salt and turmeric and mix well. Now gradually add water and mix everything well. Please make sure there are no lumps. The consistency needs to be like pancake batter.

8) Now put the batter aside for 10 minutes. Divide the potato mixture into 4 small balls.

9) Heat the oil in a *kadahi* or deep pan over a medium heat.

10) Using a spoon, dip each vada into the batter to coat the mixture.

11) Drop coated vadas in hot oil, and deep fry batter-coated balls over a medium heat until golden brown from all sides. (Tip: please drop only two vadas at a time.)

12) Once the vadas are golden and crispy, remove them with a strainer and place them on a paper towel.

13) Take one pav (bread roll) and apply red garlic chutney (page 229), mint and coriander chutney (page 228) and prune, date and tamarind chutney (page 232) on the inside of the bread. Add one vada and serve with a nice cup of masala chai (page 234).

Anda Bhurji Pav

A flavoursome quick-fix street food, yet healthy and complete when served with pav. An Indian version of scrambled eggs where the eggs are cooked and scrambled with onions, tomatoes, green chillies, ginger, some aromatic spices and, last but not least, some butter. I wish my mum could have mastered this particular dish, but because she was brought up in a Brahmin caste, she never had the liberty to venture into any exotic egg and meat dishes like this gorgeous bhurji pav. Nevertheless, I was fortunate to have the food cart stationed outside my college in Mumbai, where after intense physical training on Sundays, I could not have missed an excuse to indulge myself with this complete food to get me back on my feet.

I am sure you will love and appreciate this particular mouth-watering dish, as I did in my university days.

Ingredients (2 people)

3 large eggs

2 tbsp cooking oil

1 tbsp butter

1 medium onion, finely chopped

1 medium tomato, finely chopped

1 inch ginger, finely chopped

1–3 green spicy chilli, finely chopped (according to taste)

¼ tsp turmeric powder

½ tsp garam masala

¼ tsp ground black pepper

1 tsp coriander powder

¼ tsp chilli powder (optional)

½ tsp pav bhaji masala (see page 239)

Salt to taste

1 tbsp coriander, finely chopped

Handful spinach, finely chopped (optional – if you want to give a healthy punch)

Bread roll or a slice of any type of bread

Instructions

1) Break the eggs and add them to a mixing bowl. Whisk the eggs well.

2) Once the eggs are light and airy, put them aside. Season them with black pepper and a bit of salt.

3) Heat a non-stick pan over a medium heat and add oil and butter.

4) Once butter is melted, add finely chopped ginger and onions. Sauté them for 3–4 minutes.

5) Add chopped green chillies and tomatoes. Sauté them for 2–3 minutes.

6) Now add turmeric powder, garam masala, chilli powder, coriander powder, salt and chopped coriander and mix everything well. Put the lid on and let it cook for a minute or so.

7) Now turn the heat to low and add whisked eggs to the pan. Stir gently until the eggs are combined with onions and tomatoes.

8) Once the eggs are combined, start scrambling vigorously until the eggs are cooked perfectly and the mixture breaks into pieces. (If you are using spinach, this is the time to add chopped spinach. Mix everything well. Put the lid on and cook for a minute or so.)

9) Turn off the heat. Transfer hot bhurji to the serving bowl.

10) Serve hot with lightly toasted pav or a slice of bread.

Mumbai Cheese Masala Toast Sandwich

As the name suggests, this is a sandwich specifically originating from Bombay, as the city used to be called when I lived in India. This toasted sandwich is available at every street corner in Mumbai – from in front of schools, to near bus stops, railway stations, shopping malls, etc. The internet and social media have bridged the gaps between the sandwich and the way it's being presented by the rest of the world, and the ever-evolving and adapting Mumbai is no different. In 2018, just to tickle my taste buds and to re-live the moment, I visited one of these sandwich shops. I was amazed to see how simple ingredients such as bread, cheese, vegetables, spices and spuds were presented in fifty-plus different ways. And every sandwich had a peculiar taste and presentation. The recipe I am sharing with you is cooked by many to celebrate the start of the weekend – a common household sandwich, yet improvised by many. I am going to share the recipe for a sandwich I was brought up with. I still can't forget the smell of slightly toasted bread, very well complemented with aromatic, freshly made mint and coriander chutney and a bit of tomato ketchup.

Ingredients (3 sandwiches)

(For potato filling)

2 tbsp cooking oil

½ tsp cumin seeds

2 big potatoes, boiled and mashed

1 garlic clove, grated

½ inch ginger, grated

¼ tsp turmeric powder

½ tsp chaat masala (see page 241)

Salt to taste

1 tbsp chopped coriander

½ cup grated cheese or paneer or vegan cheese

(Other ingredients)

1 small pepper, chopped in thin rings

1 small red onion, chopped in thin rings

1 medium boiled beetroot, chopped in thin slices (optional)

1 small tomato, sliced

2 tbsp butter/ vegan butter

6 bread slices

½ tsp chaat masala

3 tsp mint and coriander chutney (page 228)

Instructions

For potato filling:

1) In a non-stick pan heat 2 tbsp oil on a medium heat.

2) When the oil is hot, add cumin seeds and sauté on a low heat.

3) When cumin seeds start releasing aroma, add grated ginger, garlic and turmeric powder. Mix well.

4) Add the boiled and mashed potatoes. Add coriander leaves, salt and chaat masala. Mix everything well.

5) Put the lid on the pan and cook for a further 2 minutes.

Methods for preparing the sandwich:

1) Spread butter on two bread slices and then mint and coriander chutney.

2) On top of one bread slice spread potato mixture. Now add 3 to 4 tomato slices, onion rings, pepper rings and beetroot slices.

3) Sprinkle 2 pinches of chaat masala. Add grated cheese or paneer. Now cover this with the other slice of bread.

4) Now spread some butter or oil in a toaster or a grill pan and toast the sandwich till it's golden and crispy. Toast on both sides.

5) Cut the masala toast sandwich into 2 or 4 pieces.

6) Finally, serve the sandwiches with some tomato ketchup and mint and coriander chutney.

> **TIP:** This sandwich can easily be made vegan. And if you don't want to use potatoes, you can always use boiled broccoli, cooked salmon or cooked chicken.

Pav Bhaji

Although I haven't lived in my city of birth for nearly two decades now, as a Mumbai girl, street food runs in my veins. I love it all, but if I have to pick one favourite, it would have to be Pav Bhaji.

Pav Bhaji is a simple fast food originated by textile workers from Mumbai. This explosively delicious dish is celebrated by many and becomes an inseparable part of every celebration. The dish, its aroma and its presentation with toasted masala pav will lift your mood whatever the weather. This, my all-time favourite street food, was introduced to me by my mother in my childhood and ever since every birthday was celebrated with pav bhaji on the side.

> **TIP:** Please don't use any other colour pepper, as green pepper not only goes well with Indian spices but also gives that unique flavour which is needed for this particular dish.

Ingredients (3 people)

2 medium size potatoes (peeled and cubed)

7–8 cauliflower florets

1 small green pepper, deseeded and chopped into cubes

3 tbsp fresh or frozen peas

4 garlic cloves, grated

½ inch ginger, peeled and grated

1 medium onion, finely chopped

2 small tomatoes, finely chopped

2 tbsp cooking oil

3 tbsp butter or vegan butter

½ tsp turmeric

1 tbsp garam masala

1½ tbsp coriander powder

2 tbsp pav bhaji masala (see page 239)

¼ -1½ tsp chilli powder (depends on how spicy you like)

2 green chillies, finely chopped (optional)

1 tbsp fresh coriander, finely chopped

2 small wedges of lime

1 small red onion, finely chopped

1 tbsp coriander, finely chopped

4 to 6 bread rolls

Instructions

1) Parboil chopped potato cubes, cauliflower florets and green pepper; alternatively, steam them for 12–15 minutes or pressure cook on high flame for 5 minutes. (If you are using a pressure cooker, add ½ cup water.)

2) Once the vegetables have cooled down, blend the mixture with a hand blender (or you can use a masher) and put it aside.

3) Heat 2 tbsp oil in a non-stick pan and add 2 tbsp butter to it.

4) When oil is hot, add grated garlic and ginger to the pan. Sauté for 30 seconds or until the raw smell of garlic is gone.

5) Now add finely chopped onions and a pinch of salt. Sauté for 10–12 minutes until the onions are light brown.

6) Add finely chopped tomatoes. Sauté for 30 seconds.

7) Now add turmeric powder, garam masala, coriander powder, pav bhaji masala and salt to taste. (If you are using green chillies, add them now.) Sauté for a minute. Add 2 tbsp water. Mix everything well.

8) Put the lid on and let the mixture cook for 2 minutes. When oil starts separating, add green peas. Mix everything and cook for a minute.

9) Now add blended vegetables to the pan. Mix well.

10) Put the lid on and let the bhaji cook on a low heat for 2 minutes.

For serving

1) Mix pav bhaji masala to butter. Spread this butter on bread rolls.

2) Grill the bread rolls on a medium heat.

3) Transfer cooked bhaji to a bowl. Add chopped coriander, red onions and a wedge of lime to the bhaji. Serve with hot toasted bread rolls.

Vegetable Schezwan (or Sichuan) Noodles

Indo-Chinese food is immensely popular in India. Among all Indo-Chinese recipes, vegetable or chicken Schezwan (or Sichuan) noodle dishes are the most preferred dishes due to their tangy, spicy and unique garlic flavour. For this utterly amazing dish, Schezwan chutney (page 231) is the key. Once you make this chutney, you can make a lot of Indo-Chinese dishes like Schezwan fried rice, chicken Schezwan curry, etc. If you are a noodle lover just like me, then you will absolutely love this recipe. Usually, Sichuan noodles are spicy but you can adjust the spice level according to your palate and taste.

Ingredients

(For cooking noodles)

150 g noodles (hakka or egg or plain)

600 ml of water (to cook noodles)

1 tbsp oil (to coat the noodles)

1 tbsp oil (to be added while boiling water)

(Other ingredients)

One small onion, finely chopped

2–3 garlic cloves, finely chopped

1 inch of ginger, peeled and finely chopped

1 small carrot, julienne or chopped in rings

2 tbsp French beans, chopped

1 small green pepper, julienne or chopped into cubes

½ cup of white cabbage, shredded

½ tsp to 2 tsp Schezwan chutney (depends how spicy you would like the food)

¼ tsp black pepper, ground

¼ tsp turmeric powder

¼ tsp to 1 tsp chilli sauce

¼ tsp garam masala

1 tbsp white or rice vinegar

1 tsp soya sauce (optional)

2 tbsp oil (for stir-frying)

1 tbsp spring onions, chopped

½ tsp sesame seeds (optional)

Salt to taste

Instructions

1) Boil 600 ml of water in a pan with ¼ tsp salt and 1 tbsp oil.

2) When the water is boiling, add the noodles.

3) Cook the noodles for about 10 minutes, or according to the package instructions.

4) When the noodles are cooked, strain the noodles in a colander.

5) Rinse the noodles very thoroughly in cold running water. This process will stop the cooking process.

6) Add oil to noodles. Toss the noodles gently, so that the oil gets coated evenly on the noodles and the noodles are not sticky.

7) Put the noodles aside and let them cool completely.

8) Heat the oil in a pan or wok on a medium heat. When the oil is hot, add garlic and ginger and sauté for a few seconds.

9) Increase the flame and then add the finely chopped onions. Stir-fry on a high heat for 40 seconds.

10) Add all the vegetables and sauté them on a high flame for about 2 to 4 minutes, until the vegetables start to become slightly brown. (You can cut down on the stir-frying time if you prefer half-cooked or more crunchy vegetables.)

11) Now reduce the flame to a medium heat and add Schezwan chutney (page 231), salt, turmeric powder, black pepper, garam masala, vinegar and soy sauce. Mix everything well.

12) Add noodles in batches and stir-fry.

13) Increase the flame and keep tossing and stir-frying the noodles till the Schezwan sauce coats all the noodles well.

14) Add chopped spring onions and sesame seeds to Schezwan noodles and stir.

15) Serve Schezwan noodles hot in a serving bowl or on a plate.

TIP: When you are adding your vegetables, please make sure that they are cooked and crunchy and not soft.

Appetizers, Snacks and Soups

- Aloo Tikki Chaat
- Vegetable Samosas Triangle and Potalis
- Railway Cutlets
- Indo-Mexican Aloo chaat
- Mulligatawny Chicken Soup
- Spinach Lentil Carrot Soup
- Tomato Shorba
- Masala Chicken Chimichanga or Chivichanga with Homemade Salsa
- Rava Prawns
- Fish Cakes
- Chicken Pakoras
- Haryali Chicken Tikka
- Turkey Momos
- Kheema Croquettes (Minced Lamb Cutlets)

Aloo Tikki Chaat

As mentioned before, one meaning of *chaat* is 'lick', but another meaning is a food item that is a sweet, tangy and spicy treat box. They are delicious, lip-smacking and must-have snacks in most Indian households. I still remember the best cook in the world, my mum, cooking tikkies more or less every weekend as evening snacks, so trust me when I say we are the experts!

Generally, chaats are enjoyed as a cheat meal on the roadside from street food hawkers or food trucks. But for chaat, I always preferred my mum's recipe. There are a lot of different types of chaats, but aloo tikki chaat with a nice cup of ginger tea (page 234) is my all-time favourite. These tikkies are easy to make and light on your tummy. So, let's get started!

> **TIPS:**
> a) You can make it vegan by adding vegan yoghurt.
> b) You can also add parboiled broccoli in potato tikki (6 to 7 florets with 3 potatoes).

Ingredients (2 people)

3 medium size potatoes (boiled, cooled and mashed)

1 red onion, finely chopped

1 tomato, finely chopped

1–3 green chillies, finely chopped (optional)

¾ cup prune, date and tamarind chutney (see page 232)

½ cup pomegranate seeds

1 tbsp honey

1½ cup thick natural or Greek yoghurt

1 tsp cumin seeds

2 tbsp coriander leaves, finely chopped

½ cup mint and coriander chutney (see page 228)

2–3 garlic cloves, grated

1 inch ginger, grated

½ cup fresh breadcrumb

1 tsp garam masala

¼ tsp turmeric powder

1 tsp coriander powder

juice of ½ lemon

¼ tsp chaat masala (see page 241)

Cooking oil

Salt to taste

Instructions

1) Take a bowl of mashed potatoes. Add turmeric powder, garam masala, coriander powder, chopped chillies, chilli powder, half a lemon juice, chopped coriander, garlic, ginger, chaat masala fresh breadcrumbs and salt to taste. Mix everything well. Put this mixture aside or in the fridge for 30 minutes.

2) Take another bowl. Add yoghurt or curd to it with honey. Mix everything and put it aside.

3) Take a pan and roast cumin seeds on a low heat for a minute or so. Please be cautious not to burn them. When they cool down, grind them with a pestle and mortar.

4) Get the potato mixture out and divide this mixture and roll the patties into a round shape. Put the non-stick pan on a hob and on a medium heat add some cooking oil. When oil is hot, add three to four patties and cook both sides until golden colour on a medium heat.

5) Once the patties are all cooked, take a plate, add whisked yoghurt or curd, mint and coriander chutney and prune, date and tamarind chutney. Now put cooked tikkies on the top.

6) Splash some yoghurt, mint and coriander chutney and prune, date and tamarind chutney. Sprinkle chopped onions, chopped tomatoes, pomegranate seeds, some chopped coriander and a pinch of chaat masala.

Vegetable Samosas Triangle and Potalis

Punjabi samosas are traditional and one of the most commonly eaten snacks across India. They are very popular as a party snack or street food and are readily available in every sweet and savoury shop or street food cart in Mumbai.

In this recipe, I made the samosa cones traditionally by using all-purpose flour to create flakiness and get that crispiness. Making a good samosa is an art and needs four very unmissable ingredients – love, patience, care and time! So I don't think there are any shortcuts to making this epic snack.

Ingredients (6–8 samosas)

(For filling)

1 medium onion, finely chopped

2 big potatoes

½ cup peas (frozen peas work best for this recipe but if you are using fresh peas, cook them until they are tender)

2 garlic cloves, finely chopped

½ inch ginger, finely chopped

1–3 green chillies, finely chopped (according to taste)

2 tbsp cashews (optional)

½ tsp garam masala

¼ tsp turmeric powder

½ tsp cumin powder

1 tsp coriander powder

½ tsp amchur powder or ½ tsp lemon juice

¼ tsp chaat masala (see page 241)

¼ tsp cumin seeds

¼ tsp coriander seeds

¼ tsp fennel seeds

1 tbsp chopped coriander leaves

2 tbsp oil for cooking

Oil for frying

(For samosa dough)

250 g all-purpose flour or plain flour

¼ tsp turmeric powder

3 tbsp ghee

¼ tsp carom seeds

Some water

Salt to taste

Instructions

1) For the dough: take a bowl and add all-purpose flour or plain flour, turmeric powder, carom seeds, salt to taste and 2 tbsp ghee. Mix flour with ghee in such a way that every grain is coated with ghee. Add water gradually and knead until you get a stiff dough. Make sure the dough is firm and pliable.

2) Cover this dough with a damp muslin cloth and put it aside.

3) Boil potatoes until tender. If you are using a pressure cooker, add 4 cups of water and ¼ tsp salt and boil potatoes with skin on. Put the lid on and pressure cook for 15 minutes or so.

4) Turn the hob off. Let pressure cooker release all the pressure. When potatoes have cooled down, take the skin off and crumble them.

5) Heat the oil in a pan on a medium heat. When oil is hot, add cumin seeds, fennel seeds and coriander seeds and turn the heat down to low. When seeds start releasing aroma, add chopped garlic, ginger and green chillies. Sauté for 30 seconds.

6) Now add finely chopped onions and sauté for 8–10 minutes. Add cashews and sauté for 30 seconds.

7) Add turmeric powder, cumin powder, amchur or lemon juice, coriander powder, chaat masala and garam masala. Mix everything well and cook for 30 to 50 seconds on a low heat.

8) Add peas, mix and cook for 30 seconds. Add mashed potatoes, chopped coriander and salt to taste. Mix everything well and let the mixture cook for a minute or so. This mixture needs to be dry, so please don't add any water.

9) Turn off the hob and put the vegetable mixture aside.

10) Divide the dough into small 5 equal parts and make small balls.

11) Take some dry flour. Roll out each ball into an oval shape (about 8 inches long and 5 inches wide).

12) Using a pizza cutter or knife, cut this oval shape into two equal semi-circular parts. These two parts will make two samosas.

13) Take one part and apply water over the cut straight edge. Join the edges to make a cone. Add water to the edges or you can use flour slurry.

14) Press down gently to seal the cone from the inside as well, otherwise your samosas will open when frying.

15) Fill this cone with vegetable mixture. (Approximately 2 tablespoons: please don't overfill it.)

16) Now coat the circular edge with water, cover over by closing and sealing coated edges of the semi-circle.

17) Repeat steps 10 to 16 for all the remaining balls. (You can create your own shapes, but please make sure that you seal the dough so that the potato filling doesn't come out of the dough – as I have done with potalis!)

18) Take a *kadahi*, wok or pan and heat 3 to 4 inches of oil.

19) When oil is hot (180°C), drop samosas, one at a time. (Please do make sure that your pan is not overcrowded.)

20) Fry samosas until they are golden brown.

21) Drain on a paper towel before serving.

22) Serve them with some leafy salad, mint and coriander chutney (page 228) and prune, date and tamarind chutney (page 232).

TIPS:

a) To get that perfect flakiness and crispiness, you must make sure that the temperature of the frying oil must be 180°C. Once the oil is smoking hot, lower the flame down to medium heat and fry your samosas.

b) You can also bake these samosas if you don't want to deep fry them. Brush some oil on the samosas and bake in a pre-heated oven (180°C) for 15 minutes.

c) To make these samosas vegan, please use any cooking oil instead of using ghee.

MAGICAL MUMBAI FLAVOURS

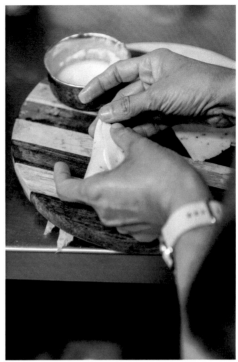

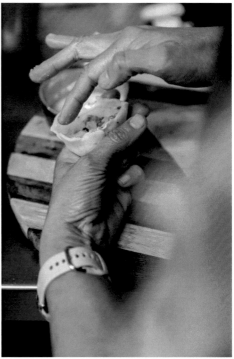

Magical Mumbai Flavours

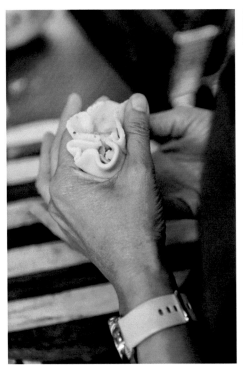

MAGICAL MUMBAI FLAVOURS

Railway Cutlets

When writing about this recipe I can still hear the sound of 'cut-less!' (the hawkers' pronunciation for 'cutlets').

In my childhood when travelling by Rajdhani express or Dehradun express trains to visit my mum and dad's family in the north of India, the real excitement was always to grab a window seat on the train rather than meeting the relatives.

Railway cutlets with masala chai were the highlight of the whole trip for me and my brother and sister. These railway cutlets are crumbed, deep-fried patties made of carrots, peas, beans, beetroot and potatoes and cut in various shapes. These patties were and still are the unmissable ritual of the train journeys in the mornings. Hard-earned money was well stretched like every other average middle-class Indian family during the 1980s and '90s. My mother used to prepare food for an anticipated long journey which then and still is two days of travelling by train, but the cutlets were one of the main attractions – not to mention the famous masala chai which I have discussed further in my book (see page 234).

The railways were introduced and established by the British to facilitate logistics and commerce for their benefit at the time of their Empire. These cutlets were the legacy of the British Raj and were thought to be one of the staple dishes on the menu in those days.

Ingredients (2–3 people)

1 small beetroot, or you can use cooked beetroot

2 large potatoes, boiled, cooled, peeled and coarsely mashed

1 small onion, finely chopped

1 tbsp French beans, finely chopped

1 small carrot, finely chopped

50 g frozen peas

3 to 4 garlic cloves, grated

1 inch ginger, grated

¼ tsp cumin seeds

200 ml oil for frying

1 to 3 green chillies (depends how spicy you like your dish to be)

¼ tsp black pepper, ground

½ tsp chaat masala (see page 241)

¼ tsp turmeric

¼ garam masala

½ tsp coriander powder

½ cup breadcrumb

¼ cup semolina (to coat the cutlets)

2 tablespoon all-purpose flour

Salt to taste

Instructions

1) Boil and mash the potatoes and put them aside.

2) Heat 3 tbsp of oil in a pan on a medium heat. When the oil is hot, add cumin seeds. When seeds start releasing aroma, add finely chopped onions and sauté for 10–15 minutes until they are light brown.

3) Add green chillies, turmeric powder, chaat masala, garam masala and coriander powder. Add frozen peas and finely chopped beetroot. Add beans and carrots and cook for 3 to 4 minutes on a low heat. Add green chillies, turmeric powder, chaat masala, garam masala and coriander powder. Mix everything well.

4) Now mix everything together. Cook on a low heat for a minute. Please make sure that there is no water in this mixture.

5) Take a potato masher and mash the mixture.

6) When the mixture cools down add mashed potatoes and fresh breadcrumbs and salt to taste. Using a potato masher, mash the mixture together: you don't want big chunks of vegetables or your cutlets will break apart when frying. Please make sure that this mixture is firm and not mushy.

7) Put some oil on your palms and make round patties or any shape you like.

8) Now take all-purpose flour in a bowl and add some water and make a flour slurry. Take a plate and add some semolina.

9) Once you have made all the cutlet shapes, dip the cutlets one by one in the flour slurry and then cover them with semolina. Keep these patties in the fridge for 30 minutes.

10) In a large non-stick pan, heat 200 ml oil for shallow frying.

11) Once the oil is hot, fry the cutlets on a medium flame until golden brown on both sides.

> **TIP:** When you dip and coat patties in slurry and semolina, always remember to use one hand to dip patties in slurry and another hand to coat patties with semolina and not breadcrumbs.

Indo-Mexican Aloo Chaat

I have always been a fan of the fusion of international cuisine with Indian cuisine. I always enjoy marrying food from two different cultures and creating a *dhamakedar* (flavour-explosive) dish. A few years ago, this dish was created in my kitchen with leftover potatoes, salsa and tortilla wraps.

There is a lot of similarity between Indian food and Mexican, i.e. use of cumin seeds, coriander seeds, chillies, black pepper, beans and rice.

I am sure you will love this particular dish as it's very close to my heart. Enjoy!

Ingredients (4 people)

(For the salsa)

2 cloves garlic, finely chopped

½ inch ginger, finely chopped

½ lime juice

1 red onion, finely chopped

1 ripe mango, chopped

2 medium tomatoes, finely chopped

2 to 3 jalapeño or green chillies, finely chopped

1 cup or 125 g of finely chopped mixed peppers (preferably green and red)

3 tbsp cooking oil

4 tbsp sweet corn, boiled

1 tbsp coriander, finely chopped

4 tbsp red kidney beans (cooked or canned)

5 tbsp tomato ketchup

1 tsp cumin powder

1 tsp garam masala

1 tsp dry oregano

2 tsp sugar

½ tsp paprika or chilli powder, optional

Salt to taste

(For Mexican masala)

4 tbsp cumin seeds

2 tbsp coriander seeds

4–5 dry red chillies

1 tbsp dry oregano

1 tbsp black peppercorns

Salt to taste

(Other ingredients)

2 medium size potatoes, boiled and cubed

2–3 tortilla wraps of your choice or leftover chapatis, cut into strips

Oil to fry potatoes and tortilla wraps or chapatis

250 g nachos (optional)

½ cup yoghurt or sour cream

Instructions

1) For the salsa: Mix all the salsa ingredients in a bowl. Put them aside.

2) Heat a pan on a medium heat. Add 3 tbsp of cooking oil. Add all the salsa ingredients and cook for 10–12 minutes on a medium heat.

3) Turn the heat off and put cooked salsa mixture aside to cool down.

4) Take a dry pan and add oil for frying potatoes and tortilla or chapati strips.

5) When the oil is hot, add potato cubes and fry them until golden brown.

6) In the same oil fry tortilla or chapati strips. Take them out when they are crispy and golden.

7) Dry roast cumin seeds, coriander seeds and the other Mexican masala ingredients. Make sure that the flame is low and roast them for a minute or so. Ground them either in a grinder or with a pestle and mortar.

8) Add 1½ tsp ground Mexican masala to fried potatoes and mix together.

9) Add 1 tsp Mexican masala to tortilla or chapati strips and mix everything well.

10) Presentation: Take a plate and add 2 tbsp salsa. Add fried potatoes and fried strips on top of salsa. Add 1 tbsp salsa. Now add nachos, then 2 tablespoons of salsa, and then 2 tbsp sour cream or yoghurt. And at the end add more Mexican masala.

Mulligatawny Chicken Soup

Mulligatawny (muh-luh-guh-taw-nee) soup came from the southern part of India and became popular worldwide. *Mullaga-Tawny* means 'pepper water'. It is an English soup inspired by an Indian recipe. It has been seen in history that whenever two cultures amalgamate, something amazing comes to life.

The British Empire ruled much of the southern parts of India and it would be quite safe to say that mulligatawny soup was the first ever Anglo-Indian culinary affair which gave the world amazing and unforgettable flavours. Now the flavour of this soup is celebrated worldwide. It was created by servants for British officers and their families who demanded a soup course from a cuisine that had never produced soup.

This soup is made of a combination of vegetables, rice, spices and/or meat. The flavours and the aroma of this specific soup are so magical that many renowned chefs have created their signature version. Here, I am going to share my love for this particular recipe.

Ingredients (3 people)

120 g boneless chicken (diced)

3 tbsp cooking oil

1 small onion, chopped

3 to 4 garlic cloves, chopped

1 bay leaf

1 inch ginger, chopped

1 to 4 green chillies, chopped (according to taste)

1 tsp garam masala

¼ tsp cumin powder

1½ coriander powder

¾ tsp turmeric powder

¼ tsp to 1 tsp black pepper

½ cup red lentils (masoor dal), washed and drained

3 tbsp rice, washed and drained

1 small carrot, chopped

1 medium potato, peeled and chopped

1 apple, peeled, cored and chopped

1 tsp lemon juice

1 cup coconut milk

1 cup vegetable stock or water

1 tbsp fresh coriander leaves, finely chopped

Salt to taste

Instructions

1) Heat the oil in a pan on a medium heat. Once the oil is hot, add bay leaf, chopped garlic and ginger. When the raw smell of garlic is gone, add chopped onions and chopped green chillies. Sauté them until onions become translucent (roughly 8 to 9 minutes).

2) Now add turmeric, coriander powder, garam masala, ground black pepper and cumin powder. Add a splash of water and mix everything together.

3) Now add the diced chicken, rice, lentils and carrot, apple, potatoes and vegetable stock to a pan. Mix everything together. Cook and simmer for about 20 to 25 minutes on a low heat until chicken, rice and vegetable are cooked. Keep checking and, if necessary, add some water.

4) Once the chicken, rice and lentils are cooked and the vegetables are tender, turn off the hob. Let this mixture cool down and take the bay leaf out.

5) Blend the mixture in a food processor until puréed.

6) Heat 1 tbsp oil in a pan on a medium heat. When the oil is hot, add cumin seeds, then after 30 seconds add puréed mixture, coconut milk, salt to taste and chopped coriander leaves.

7) Eat with your favourite bread roll or with plain rice.

> **TIP**: If you don't like adding chicken or any other meat you can either use potatoes or soya chunks which are easily available in Indian shops or online.

Spinach Lentil Carrot Soup

Soup – The best way to warm anyone up on a cold winter day, don't you think? I call this soup a complete, fresh, and healthful soup because there are three amazing and very nutritious ingredients: red lentils, carrots and spinach. When they are cooked together with some aromatic spices, they give you a gratifying taste. This is a simple and quick recipe. Red split lentils are easily available in many shops.

One of my granddads, who was an Ayurvedic doctor, always claimed that lentils are not only cheap and a good source of protein but are also good for your body and environment. He also believed that these kinds of simple food offer your digestion a much-needed rest from a daily routine bogged down by stress and complex food.

Ingredients (3 people)

200 g spinach

65 g red split lentils, washed and soaked for at least 30 minutes

2 medium carrots, chopped

1 small onion, chopped

2 garlic cloves, finely chopped

1 inch ginger, chopped

¼ tsp cumin seeds

½ tsp turmeric powder

¼ tsp honey (optional)

¼ tsp black pepper, ground

5 tbsp oil

¼ tsp asafoetida

1 tbsp fresh coriander leaves

Salt to taste

Instructions

1) Heat 3 tbsp oil in a pan on a medium heat.
2) When oil is hot, add cumin seeds and asafoetida.
3) When cumin seeds go brown and you can smell its earthy aromas, add chopped garlic and sauté for 30 seconds.
4) Add chopped onions and sauté and cook until golden brown.
5) Now add turmeric powder and mix everything well.
6) Add chopped carrots and washed lentils. Mix everything together.
7) Add 450ml water and cook until lentils are cooked.
8) Add 250ml water and spinach. Cook for a further 2 minutes.

9) Turn off the hob and let everything cool down.
10) Blend this mixture with a hand blender to a smooth thin purée.
11) Heat one tbsp oil on a medium heat. Add blended lentils and carrots.
12) Add honey (optional), ground black pepper and salt to taste. Cook for a further 2 minutes.
13) Turn off the hob. Serve this soup hot with either chapati or soup bread.

Tomato Shorba

Shorba is the kind of soup that has roots connected with ancient Persia and arrived in India along with the Mughals. Shorba is derived from the Arabic word *Shurba*. Shorba can be made in various ways. Traditionally, they were mainly meat shorbas which were bought by the Mughals but when they arrived in India, it was transformed to suit vegetarian and vegan diets too. My memory of enjoying this simple yet flavoursome soup is when my mum used to make it during winter and I used to enjoy it with a bowl of rice. You might be thinking, 'Are you serious! Soup with rice??'

Yes, this spiced tomato soup is different from the regular tomato soup. Soup is usually served as a starter, but this tomato shorba can be and is served in many households in India as an accompaniment to the main dishes. It is a lightened-up version of a classic tomato soup. It may look remarkably similar to tomato soup, but it's a great fusion of herbs and spices that gives shorba that distinctive flavour.

Ingredients (3 people)

3 medium firm tomatoes (roughly chopped)

1 tbsp cooking oil

¼ tsp cumin seeds

1 small bay leaf

2 garlic cloves, finely chopped

½ inch ginger, peeled and finely chopped

¼ tsp turmeric powder

¼ tsp garam masala

½ tsp coriander powder

1 tbsp chopped coriander powder

1½ cup vegetable stock or water

Salt to taste

Instructions

1) Take chopped tomatoes and blend them without adding any water. Blend till smooth.

2) Put tomato purée aside.

3) Heat 1 tablespoon of oil in a pan on a medium heat.

4) When oil is hot, add a bay leaf and cumin seeds.

5) When cumin seeds go brown and you can smell its earthy aromas, add chopped ginger and garlic. Sauté for 30 seconds.

6) Now add the tomato purée. Stir and simmer for 2 minutes on a low heat.

7) Let everything cook for 2 minutes.

8) Now add turmeric powder, chilli powder, coriander powder, garam masala and ground black pepper.

9) Mix everything well.

10) Add 2 cups of vegetable stock or just water.

11) Add some salt and simmer tomato shorba on a low to medium flame for 4 to 5 minutes.

12) Turn off the hob and add chopped coriander leaves.

13) Serve hot as soup or as a side dish with any rice dish.

Masala Chicken Chimichanga (or Chivichanga) with Homemade Salsa

For me, this chimichanga is an all-round healthy meal on the go. During the lockdown, when Dalvi's restaurant was opened just for takeaways, it was the most popular food item on a sharing platter. So, I thought I would share the crowd-pleasing and cheering recipe of Dalvi's Chimichanga with the rest of the world. It is the easiest recipe. Believe me, you and your loved ones will love it. Chicken chimichanga – a tortilla filled with some vegetables, red kidney beans, pulled chicken and cheese – is not only a quick meal but also full of sharp flavours which summon your taste buds on the first bite. (The salsa recipe is the same as for Indo-Mexican aloo chaat on page 71.)

> **TIP:** If you like you can make it vegetarian too by adding paneer or vegetables of your choice instead of chicken.

Ingredients (4 people)

(For salsa)

2 cloves garlic, finely chopped

½ inch ginger, finely chopped

½ lime juice

1 red onion, finely chopped

1 ripe mango, chopped

2 medium tomatoes, finely chopped

2 to 3 jalapeño or green chillies, finely chopped

1 cup or 125 g of finely chopped mixed peppers (preferably green and red)

3 tbsp cooking oil

4 tbsp sweet corn, boiled

1 tbsp coriander, finely chopped

4 tbsp red kidney beans (cooked or canned)

5 tbsp tomato ketchup

1 tsp cumin powder

1 tsp garam masala

1 tsp dry oregano

2 tsp sugar

½ tsp paprika or chilli powder, optional

Salt to taste

(For chicken marinade)

3 garlic cloves, grated

1 inch of ginger, grated

300 g chicken (boneless)

2 tbsp yoghurt

1 tsp garam masala

½ tsp cumin powder

1 tsp coriander powder

¼ tsp black pepper, ground

Salt to taste

(For cooking)

3 tbsp cooking oil

75 g mixed peppers, thinly sliced

1 red onion, thinly sliced

¼ tsp ground black pepper

Marinated chicken

Salt to taste

(For chimichanga pockets)

4 tortillas of your choice

Mozzarella cheese, grated

Cooking oil for frying

(For serving)

Prepared salsa

Cooked chicken and vegetables

Sour cream

Instructions

Marination:

1) Take a bowl and add all the marinade ingredients. Mix everything well. Cover with cling film and keep the marinated chicken in the fridge for an hour.

Salsa:

2) Mix all the salsa ingredients in a bowl. Put them aside.

3) Heat a pan on a medium heat. Add 3 tbsp of cooking oil. Add all the salsa ingredients and cook for 10–12 minutes on a medium heat.

4) Turn the heat off and put cooked salsa mixture aside to cool down.

Cooking chicken:

5) Heat the oil in a saucepan on a medium heat. When oil is hot, add thinly sliced onions and marinated chicken. Mix everything together and if necessary, add a splash of water. Let the chicken cook for 20 minutes or so or until it is cooked thoroughly. If needed add a splash of water so that chicken does not get burnt.

6) To make pulled chicken, use a fork to pull the chicken apart once it is cooked and has cooled down.

Assembling:

7) Take a tortilla wrap of your choice. Add 1 tbsp salsa sauce in the centre and then add 1–2 tbsp pulled chicken. Now add 1 tbsp grated cheese

8) Bring all four sides, overlap them and make them into a pillow.

9) Take a grill pan and add 2 tsp oil. When oil is hot, add two chimichangas to the pan on a low heat. Cook both sides until they are crispy and golden brown.

10) Serve with sour cream on top and with salsa sauce.

Rava Prawns

What can I say – a great accompaniment to beer! This takes me back to my first ever holidays in Goa after becoming Mrs Dalvi. Rava prawns bring back memories of this lovely beach hut near Palolem beach where after a midday swim I was greeted with chilled beer and rava prawns from the menu. This was the first time I ever tasted beer. India is slowly embracing Western openness only in cities but in my early 20s a girl drinking alcohol was a taboo in my society. Anyway, let's move on!

This is one of the popular and must-have prawn dishes at Dalvi's Restaurant. If you love seafood, try this crunchy and flavoursome Goan-style *jhinga* (prawn) recipe. It is a traditional Goan dish where marinated prawns are coated with rava (semolina) and deep-fried to give that exquisite flavour. Goan *thali* is never complete without rava fried delicacies.

Ingredients (3–4 people)

16–18 prawns (medium tiger prawns)

¾ of turmeric powder

5–6 garlic cloves & 2 inches of ginger, grated

1 tbsp lemon juice

½ tsp to 2 tsp chilli powder or paprika (according to taste)

1 tsp coriander powder

Salt to taste

2 eggs, beaten

50 g semolina (rava)

Oil for deep frying

Instructions

1) Remove the head, shell and intestine of the prawns.

2) Marinade the prawns with grated ginger and garlic, turmeric powder, red chilli powder, coriander powder, lemon juice and salt.

3) Keep the prawns in the fridge and marinade them for at least 15 minutes.

4) In a small bowl, break the egg and whisk.

5) In another bowl, mix semolina with a bit of salt and ground black pepper. Mix everything well.

6) Take the marinated prawns, coat them with beaten egg and then the semolina mix. Keep them in the fridge for at least 10 minutes.

7) Take a *kadahi* (or a pan or wok). Add oil for deep frying.

8) Once the oil is hot, add semolina-coated prawns in the oil. Please don't overcrowd your pan.

9) Fry the prawns for 2 to 3 minutes or until they are cooked.

10) Serve hot with mint and coriander chutney (page 228).

Fish Cakes

The best thing about having friends from many corners of India is that you always have the pleasure of tasting some outstanding regional dishes. How can I forget Anita, my friend who always used to bring fish cakes for me as she knew I wasn't allowed to eat seafood or meat? The recipe I am sharing here is from my friend Anita's mum.

These fish cakes are immensely popular when they are on the restaurant menu. And now I am sure they are going to be famous, loved and cherished in your household, wherever you are.

Ingredients (4 people)

100 g salmon fish or king fish (oily fish)

100 g cooked hake fish or cod fish (white fish)

3 to 4 medium size baking or white potatoes

2 inches of ginger, grated

2–3 garlic cloves, grated

1 to 3 green chillies, finely chopped (according to taste)

½ tsp lemon juice

½ tsp cumin seeds

½ tsp coriander seeds

½ tsp or onion seeds (kalonji)

1½ tsp garam masala

1 tsp turmeric powder

2 tsp coriander powder

¼ tsp to 2 tsp chilli powder

½ tsp chaat masala (see page 241)

1 tbsp mint, finely chopped

2 tbsp coriander, finely chopped

Salt to taste

½ cup all-purpose flour

¼ tsp black pepper

1 cup semolina

Cooking oil for shallow frying

Instructions

1) Boil potatoes with a skin on in a pan for 30 minutes.

2) Heat a pan on a medium heat. Add 2 to 3 tbsp oil, add fish and cook them for 6–8 minutes until they are cooked on both sides.

3) Take a bowl. Add mashed potatoes, fish and all the other ingredients except all-purpose flour, semolina and cooking oil. Combine everything well.

4) Now, make patties depending on how large you want them to be and set aside to chill in the fridge for 30 minutes.

5) Take another bowl. Add all-purpose flour, ¼ tsp black pepper and salt to taste. Mix everything together. Add ¼ cup water gradually to make slurry. But please don't make this slurry too watery.

6) Dip patties into the slurry with one hand, and then dip it in the semolina, making sure to coat all around with another hand. By doing this you will have dry semolina. Repeat this process for all patties.

7) Heat 6 to 8 tbsp oil in a pan on a medium heat. Add 3 to 4 patties at a time. Cook both sides for 2 to 3 minutes on a low to medium heat until they look golden brown.

8) Sprinkle chaat masala and serve with mint and coriander chutney (page 228) or apple cinnamon chutney.

> **TIPS:**
> 1) When dipping the patties, please make sure that you don't mix your working hands. If it's me working, I will use my left hand to dip patties in a slurry, throw those patties in a bowl of semolina and use my right hand to cover it with semolina.
>
> 2) When boiling potatoes, boil them with skin on as the skin has nutrition and with skin on potatoes don't soak a lot of water.

Chicken Pakoras

Three words for this chicken pakoras recipe – easy, delightful, contenting!

A perfect recipe if you are having friends around or having an easy night or for a special night or parties – whatever the reason is. These little crispy and luscious pakoras are another popular dish not only in Dalvi's Restaurant but also in the Dalvi household.

There are various recipes for these but the one I am sharing here is the way my sister-in-law cooks them for us. You can make these pakoras mild for the children too. My son Aadhritt (aged seven) affirmed them to be the best and he prefers them to fried chicken. I am sure you will enjoy this recipe.

Ingredients (2 people)

(For marinade)

170 g chicken breast, sliced as strips

½ tsp ginger/ garlic paste

¼ tsp turmeric powder

1 tbsp yoghurt

Salt to taste

½ tsp mixed herbs

(For batter)

6 tbsp besan (gram flour)

½ tsp garam masala

1 tsp coriander powder

2 pinches of Dalvi's Magic Masala* (optional)

¼ tsp turmeric powder

Salt to taste

Water to make batter (pancake consistency)

Oil to fry chicken pakoras

> **TIP:** Instead of using water you can use beer as that will make pakoras crispier. Please do not use heavily flavoured or dark beer for the batter.

---

* Available to buy from Dalvi's restaurant.

Instructions

1) Take a bowl and marinade chicken with all the marinade ingredients. Keep in the fridge for half an hour to 2 hours.

2) Take another bowl, add besan (gram flour) and all the other ingredients under 'For batter' and mix well.

3) Add water or beer gradually to make a batter. (The consistency should be slightly thicker than pancake batter.)

4) Take a pan or *kadahi* and add oil to deep fry pakoras.

5) Batter marinated chicken and fry it in hot oil. (Make sure oil is hot.)

6) When they turn golden, transfer them to a serving plate. (Please check whether the chicken is cooked. You can always use a probe to check the temperature.)

7) Eat it with some leafy salad and apple & beetroot chutney (page 227) and raita.

Haryali Chicken Tikka

Haryali or green chicken tikkas are the most amazing, tender and juicy tikkas which not only simply melt in your mouth but also satisfy your soul.

Grill them in a grill pan or in the oven or outdoor BBQ and believe me, these Haryali tikkas will surely rock your evenings or your parties and will become your new grilling favourite. These tikkas taste divine with beetroot & apple chutney and mint and coriander chutney.

Ingredients (4 people)

300 g chicken thighs, cut into medium-size pieces

½ tsp ginger paste (or you can grate 1-inch fresh ginger)

½ tsp garlic paste (or you can grate 3 garlic cloves)

¼ -1 tsp green chillies, finely chopped, or ¼ -1 tsp chilli powder

¼ tsp black pepper, ground

2 tbsp thick Greek yoghurt

1 cup spinach, blanched and puréed

2 tbsp double cream

1 tbsp coriander, finely chopped

½ tsp garam masala

¼ tsp lemon juice

Salt to taste

25 g butter

1 tbsp oil

1 small onion, cut into rings

> **TIP:** Blanching spinach: Dip washed spinach leaved in hot water for a minute and then transfer these leaves into ice cold water for 30 seconds. This process keeps the colour of spinach fresh green when you make a purée by using a blender.

Instructions

1) Take a bowl and add all the ingredients excluding butter, oil and onion. Mix everything well and now add diced chicken thighs.

2) Cover the bowl and keep marinated chicken in the fridge for 30 minutes to 2 hours or preferably overnight.

3) Soak wooden skewers in water for 10 minutes. Shake off the excess marinade and thread the marinated chicken pieces onto the skewers, leaving enough space between the pieces for the heat to penetrate.

4) If you are using a grill oven, preheat the grill on a high setting. Place skewered chicken on a wire rack on the top shelf.

5) Cook under the grill for 10 to 15 minutes. Apply some melted butter every five minutes and cook until the juice runs clear and the chicken is cooked through and slightly charred around the edges.

6) If you are using a grill pan, heat the pan on a medium heat. When the pan is hot, add 1 tablespoon of oil and butter.

7) Once butter is melted, add chicken skewers and turn the hob to low to medium heat. After 3–4 minutes, flip them and cook for a further 4 minutes. Cook both sides until the chicken is cooked through.

8) Take the chicken off the skewers. Rest them either on leafy salad or naan. Sprinkle chaat masala on them and serve with mint & coriander chutney and onion rings.

Turkey Momos

My love affair with momos, or dim sum, began when I was on an organised school trip to one of my favourite countries, Nepal in July 2012.

A beautiful late afternoon and we were about to wrap up for the day. Fortunately, should I say, we were caught up in the rain which forced us to take refuge in a nearby beautiful local café by the river. That was the time when I was introduced to the local delicacy of chicken momos for the first time. The momos were served with spicy chilli sauce, which was catered for locals and I must say it was very spicy. Whilst writing this recipe, I could still taste those heavenly momos along with the smell of earthy aromas caused by the short spell of rain.

During my recent visits to Mumbai, I was surprised and happy to see a variety of momos as street food by local restaurants and local food carts.

Momos, originating from Tibet, are a very versatile food for which momo chutney is a must. The filling for momos can be vegetarian, minced chicken or lamb or goat meat; I am sharing a minced turkey here as this is very popular in the Dalvi household.

Ingredients

(For the turkey filling)

125 g minced turkey

½ cup red onion, finely chopped

½ tsp garlic, finely chopped

¼ tsp ginger, finely chopped

¼ tsp green chillies, finely chopped

½ tsp soya sauce

¼ tsp white vinegar

¼ tsp black pepper, ground

1 tbsp oil

Salt to taste

(For the dough)

150 g all-purpose flour

½ tsp baking powder

Salt to taste

¼ tsp turmeric (optional – just for the colour)

(For the momo chutney)

1 small red onion, chopped

2 small tomatoes, chopped

6–8 dry red chillies

8–10 garlic cloves

5–6 black peppercorns

Salt to taste

4–5 tbsp cooking oil

1 tbsp coriander, finely chopped

½ -1 tsp chilli powder (optional)

¼ tsp soy sauce

½ tsp white vinegar

Instructions

1) Take a bowl and mix all the ingredients mentioned under the 'turkey filling' heading.

2) Take another bowl and knead the all-purpose flour, baking powder and salt together into a firm dough. Cover and keep aside for 20 minutes.

3) Roll the dough into very thin 3-inch rounds.

4) Now take each round piece and place some turkey filling in the centre.

5) Now sprinkle some water on the edges and bring both edges together and stick them.

6) Now grab 2 corners and stick them together.

7) Steam in a steamer for about 10–15 minutes.

8) Turn off the steamer, wait for a few minutes and let the steamer settle.

For momo chutney:

9) Soak red chillies in hot water for 15 minutes.

10) Heat cooking oil in a pan on a medium heat. Add onions and sauté them for 2 to 3 minutes.

11) Add garlic, black peppercorns and tomatoes. Mix everything together and sauté them for a minute or so.

12) Take the chillies out of the water and add them to the pan. Add salt to taste and cook for a further 3 to 4 minutes.

13) Add chilli sauce, chilli powder, ¼ tsp soy sauce and ¼ tsp white vinegar. Mix everything and cook for a further 2 minutes.

14) Turn off the hob and let the momo chutney cool down. Blend this mixture into a chutney. Add chopped coriander and mix. (This chutney can be kept in the fridge for at least 2 months.)

15) Serve hot momos with momo chutney and some salad.

Kheema Croquette (or Minced Lamb Cutlets)

I was, and am, blessed to have a lot of amazing cooks, or should I say home chefs, in my life, like my husband, my nan, my mum, my dad, my mother-in-law, my grandmother-in-law, my sisters-in-law, and my aunties – the list is endless. The food always tasted and still tastes heavenly, because the main ingredients were, and are always, love, patience and passion for the food.

Lean goat meat cutlets were introduced to me by Krish's nan, an amazing lady who was beautiful inside and out and was a whirlwind at the age of 80. (I wish I have the same energy when I am that age.) She had a gifted sense of taste and smell and she could tell what was missing from your curries by looking at them and having a good sniff. Her mutton cutlets were to die for and immensely popular, so that all her neighbours used to come to her to get the cutlet spice mix, as this spice mix always brings out the flavours in mutton cutlets.

When it is cooked in my household, we use minced lamb as it is a bit difficult to get lean goat meat. But the taste is to die for. I am sharing a recipe of Krish's nan, with a twist of minced lamb.

Ingredients (4 people)

200 g minced lamb

1 small red onion, finely chopped

1 tsp garlic purée (or grated 3 garlic cloves)

½ tsp ginger purée (or grated 1 inch ginger)

1 to 4 green chillies, finely chopped (as per your taste)

1 tsp lemon juice

2 tbsp yoghurt

1 tbsp mint leaves, finely chopped

1 tbsp fresh coriander leaves, finely chopped

1 tsp garam masala

1½ tsp coriander power

½ tsp turmeric powder

¼ tsp black pepper, ground

¼ tsp Dalvi's Magic Masala* (optional)

½ tsp chaat masala (see page 241)

½ tsp cumin seeds

½ tsp funnel seeds

½ tsp coriander seeds

1 medium potato, boiled and mashed

½ cup breadcrumb

2 eggs, beaten

Salt to taste

Oil for frying

* Available to buy from Dalvi's restaurant.

Instructions

1) Take a pan and on a low heat roast cumin seeds, funnel seeds and coriander seeds. Once the aroma starts realising, turn off the hob and empty these seeds into a bowl.

2) In this bowl, add finely chopped onions, green chillies, mint, coriander, lemon juice, yoghurt, mint leaves, coriander leaves, all the spices and salt. Mix everything well.

3) Now add mashed potato and minced lamb. Mix everything well.

4) Cover the bowl and put it in the fridge for 30 minutes to an hour or preferably overnight.

5) Take the bowl out of the fridge and make small round patties (approximately 1.5 inches). Coat the patties with beaten egg first and then the breadcrumb mix. Keep them in the fridge for a further 10 minutes.

6) Take a *kadahi* or a pan or a wok. Add oil for deep frying.

7) Once the oil is hot, add lamb patties into it, 2 to 3 at a time.

8) On a medium heat, fry the patties for 3 to 5 minutes on both sides or until they are cooked. Keep moving the patties so that they don't stick to the bottom. Once they are golden brown and the lamb is cooked, take them out.

9) Serve hot with mint & coriander chutney and some small onion rings.

TIPS:

a) You can shallow fry them if you prefer. Please make sure that the patties are slightly flatter so that the lamb gets cooked through.

b) If you don't like minced lamb, you can replace this with minced chicken or vegetables of your choice.

Main Curries

- Dalvi's Mixed Vegetable Curry
- Channa Masala with Potatoes
- Rajma Chawal
- Nan's Potato Curry
- Chicken Curry with a hint of Spinach
- Dhaba Chicken
- Butter Chicken
- Butter Chicken Pizza
- Malwani Chicken
- Malai Kadahi Chicken Dalvi's Style
- Kerala-style Lamb Curry
- Mangshor Jhol Lamb
- Minced lamb Kofta Curry
- Prawn Masala
- Dalvi's Salmon Curry
- Red Snapper Fish Saar

Dalvi's Mixed Vegetable Curry
(Can be made vegan too)

As the name suggests, this is a very popular household curry in India. Most of the time, at home we are left with chunks of vegetables and always the question is, what do we do? Both my mum and my mother-in-law used to put them together: never mind their flavours, but with simple spices, the curry used to taste divine.

This is a simple but very flavoursome curry that goes well with chapati or pooris or rice, or even a slice of bread. The best thing about this curry is you can use any vegetable you find in your kitchen and make a one-pot, delicious and healthy curry.

> **TIPS:**
> a) When using store-bought paneer, dip the chunks in warm salty water before adding to the gravy. It softens the paneer and allows it to absorb the gravy more easily.
> b) If you are vegan, you can replace the paneer with tofu.

Ingredients (2 people)

2 to 3 tbsp cooking oil

½ tsp cumin seeds

1 bay leaves

½ inch cinnamon stick

1 medium onion, finely chopped

1 medium tomato, finely chopped

30 g fresh or frozen peas

1 medium potato, small thinly sliced

50 g paneer, cut into cubes (optional)

3 to 4 small broccoli florets

3 to 4 small cauliflower florets

Handful green French beans, chopped

½ tsp garam masala

1 tsp coriander powder

¼ tsp to 2 tsp chilli powder (depends how spicy you like)

½ tsp turmeric powder

¼ tsp Dalvi's Magic Masala* (optional)

Some water

1 tbsp fresh coriander leaves, finely chopped

Salt to taste

* Available to buy from Dalvi's restaurant.

Instructions

1) Heat the oil in a frying pan. When the oil is hot, add cinnamon stick, bay leaf and cumin seeds. Add whole red chillies if you like it spicy.

2) When cumin seeds start releasing their aroma, add the onions. Stir and cook the onions until they turn translucent (about 10 minutes). Add grated ginger and garlic and cook for 30 seconds.

3) Add chopped tomatoes, mix well with onions and add garam masala, coriander powder, turmeric powder, chilli powder and a bit of salt.

4) Mix everything, add a sprinkle of water and cover the pan and let it cook for a minute or so on a low to medium heat or until the oil separates.

5) Add potatoes, all the vegetables and ¼ cup of water, mix everything and put the lid on. Let it cook for 12–15 minutes on a low heat.

6) Keep checking occasionally and, if necessary, add a splash of water.

7) Check whether vegetables are cooked. If not, cook for a further few minutes. If necessary, add a splash of water.

8) Once the vegetables are cooked, add paneer or tofu, chopped coriander and Dalvi's Magic Masala. Mix everything well. Cook for a further 2 minutes.

9) Serve with haryali pooris (page 187) or masala laccha paratha (page 195).

Channa Masala with Potatoes Curry
(Can be made vegan too)

This curry is remarkably close to my heart because this is the first curry I cooked in a clay pot with my nan, my best friend. This simple yet truly mouth-watering curry was one of the many recipes up my nan's sleeve. It's amazing how cooking her recipes always takes me back to the memories of our time spent together in a typical Indian *rasoi* (kitchen) and brings afresh all the best times I spent with her. Is it wrong to say that sometimes I do feel her presence near me and that brings a big smile to my face and happy tears? I am sure I am making her immensely proud when she looks down from heaven as I am passionately following my dream as a self-made chef.

Chickpea curry is a favourite curry dish in most Indian households. Usually, they buy dry chickpeas, soak them for a few hours or overnight and then pressure-cook them. That's exactly what I have done for this recipe. But you can use a tin of cooked and ready-to-use chickpeas too for this recipe.

Ingredients (2–3 people)

400 g tin of cooked chickpeas (or 250 g of dry chickpeas, washed and soaked in hot water for 6–8 hours)

2 small onions, finely chopped

2 small tomatoes, finely chopped

6 to 8 baby potatoes or 2 medium potatoes (parboiled)

1 inch ginger, finely chopped or grated or ½ tsp ginger paste

2 to 3 garlic cloves, finely chopped or grated or ½ tsp garlic paste

1 bay leaf

1–2 green chillies

1 inch cinnamon stick

¼ tsp cumin seeds

½ tsp turmeric powder

¾ tsp garam masala

1½ tsp coriander powder

¼ tsp to 2 tsp chilli powder (depends how spicy you like)

½ tsp cumin powder

¼ tsp black pepper, ground

1 tbsp coriander leaves, finely chopped

¼ tsp Dalvi's Magic Masala* (optional)

Salt to taste

3 tbsp cooking oil

---

*　Available to buy from Dalvi's restaurant.

Instructions

1) If you are using a pressure cooker, add your soaked chickpeas and add 4 cups of water. Add salt and mix everything. Put the lid on and cook on a high heat for 5–10 minutes. After that, turn the heat down to a low to medium heat and cook your chickpeas for a further 15 to 20 minutes. Turn off the heat and let the pressure cooker cool down.

2) Heat the oil in a frying pan. When the oil is hot, add cinnamon stick, bay leaf and cumin seeds. Add chopped green chillies if you like your curry to be spicy.

3) When cumin seeds start realising aromas, add the onions, stir and cook the onions until the onions are light brown (about 10–15 minutes). Add grated ginger and garlic or ginger and garlic paste and cook for 30 seconds.

4) Add chopped tomatoes, mix well with onions and add garam masala, coriander powder, turmeric powder, chilli powder and a bit of salt.

5) Mix everything, add a sprinkle of water and cover the pan and let it cook for 30 seconds or until oil separates.

6) Add chickpeas, mix everything and add a splash of water.

7) Cover the pan and simmer until everything is cooked – about 10–12 minutes.

8) Meanwhile, take a frying pan or a grill pan and 2 tbsp oil. Add salt and ¼ of black pepper. Add boiled potatoes and toss them in a pan. Cook them on a low-medium heat. When potatoes are golden brown, turn the heat off.

9) Add the potatoes and Dalvi's Magic Masala and mix them with chickpeas. Cook for a minute or so.

10) Add chopped coriander leaves.

11) Serve with naan or chapatis or rice.

> **TIP:** If you don't want potatoes you can either add sweet potatoes or skip potatoes completely.

> **RESEARCH** – According to recent research, it is proved that turmeric with black pepper has a great effect on inflammation, digestion, reducing pain and fighting cancer.

Rajma Chawal
(Can be made vegan too)

Everywhere in the world, people love weekends and so did I in my childhood days and still do as a restaurant owner when I am orchestrating Dalvi's restaurant and running its kitchen. In my childhood, I used to wait eagerly for Sundays as they were special to me because of my love for rajma chawal. Rajma (curried red kidney beans) with chawal (steamed basmati rice) is one of the most loved North Indian curries, cooked in an onion and tomato mixture with Indian spices. As my parents are from the north of India, this dish was always a family favourite when I used to live with my parents back in Mumbai.

As I mentioned for the chickpea curry on the previous pages, you can either soak some kidney beans for a few hours and then pressure cook them or you can buy a tin of ready to use kidney beans. This recipe is dedicated to my awesome mum who never got tired of feeding three very hungry children. I always try my best to live up to my mum's standard of cooking rajma because her rajma chawal is the best in the whole wide world.

> **TIPS:**
> a) For me, good rajma should not only just be flavourful but also have a melt-in-the-mouth texture. The gravy of rajma should be on the slightly thicker side.
> b) If you are using a pressure cooker for this curry, soak 400 g kidney beans in warm water for 6–8 hours or overnight, drain off the water and add them to a pressure cooker with 5 cups or 1.25l of water and salt. Secure the lid, cook for 10 minutes on a high heat, then turn the heat down to low to a medium heat and cook for 25 minutes (for 4–5 whistles).
> c) If you are vegan, you can use vegan butter in place of ghee.
> d) If you don't like using red kidney beans you can substitute them with pinto beans.

Ingredients (3–4 people)

400 g of tinned kidney beans (or dried beans – see 'Tips' on previous page)

3 medium onions (grind them to make a purée)

3 medium tomatoes (grind them to make a purée)

4 to 6 tbsp cooking oil.

3–4 garlic cloves, grated, or 1 tsp garlic paste

2 inches of ginger, peeled and grated, or ½ tsp ginger paste

1 to 4 green chillies, finely chopped (optional)

½ tsp turmeric powder

2½ tsp garam masala

1 tsp cumin powder

4 tsp coriander powder

¼ to 2 tsp chilli powder (depends on the spice level you like)

Salt to taste

1 tbsp fresh coriander, finely chopped

25 g of butter or ghee

Instructions

1) Heat the oil in a pan on a medium heat. When the oil is hot, add grated ginger and garlic and sauté for a minute or so. Stirring constantly, until the garlic loses its raw smell.

2) Now add puréed onion and a pinch of salt. Put the lid on and cook for 15–20 minutes on a low heat until the onion loses its raw smell and starts changing colour.

3) Add puréed tomatoes and all the spices. Mix everything well, add ½ cup of water and let this mixture cook for 3 to 4 minutes or until you can see the oil start to separate around the edges.

4) Add kidney beans along with their liquid. Mix everything well. Simmer for about 15 minutes, until the liquid has thickened. If necessary, add some water gradually.

5) Now turn the heat off and add ghee or butter and finely chopped coriander to the curry. Mix everything well.

6) Serve with Chawal or rice and aloo paneer triangle paratha (page 193).

Nan's Potato Curry
(Suitable for vegan)

My nan – my best friend – was born and brought up in a small village in Northern India. When I was young, the only time we could visit my nan was during the hot Indian summer holidays, in the months of April to June. At the time, the Indian railway was the only transport link available between my family and my nan's residence. Nowadays, you have got better options and transport links available to arrive at a particular time, but as far as I remember we always arrived at supper time. I am talking about the times when electricity was a novelty and the whole village was deprived of such novelty at the time. Nevertheless, seeing that beautiful face always cheered me up. And once we had arrived at my nan's, she always used to cook something fresh, or should we say 'straight from the oven'. And her quick fix to get us out of 36 hours of travel fatigue was her mouth-watering delicious potato curry with pooris and plain rice.

Whenever this curry is on the restaurant menu it is always a popular dish. Often our guests say, "How did you make this potato curry so divine?" I always look at them with a smile and say, "Because it is my nan's recipe."

Ingredients (4 people)

3 medium size potatoes, boiled

2 medium onions, grated

1 tomato, grated

2 tbsp cooking oil

1 to 3 green chillies (optional)

¼ tsp cumin seeds

2 pinches of carom seeds

A pinch of asafoetida (hing) (optional)

1 tsp garam masala

½ tsp turmeric powder

3 tsp coriander powder

¼ tsp ginger powder

¼ tsp to 2 tsp chilli powder (depends on how spicy you like your curry to be)

½ tsp fennel seed powder or ½ tsp fennel seeds

¼ tsp amchoor powder or lemon juice

1 tbsp fresh coriander, finely chopped

1 tsp kasuri methi (dry fenugreek leaves)

Instructions

1) Heat the oil in a pan on a medium heat. When the oil is hot, add asafoetida, cumin seeds and carom seeds and let them crackle for a few seconds.

2) Add green chillies and cook for 20 seconds. Add grated onions and a pinch of salt. Cook for 10 to 12 minutes until the raw smell of onion is gone.

3) Now add grated tomatoes, turmeric, chilli powder, coriander powder, fennel seeds powder or fennel seeds, amchoor powder or lemon juice, garam masala and ginger powder. Mix everything well.

4) Cook on a low heat and until the oil separates from the side.

5) Break the boiled potatoes using fingers roughly and add them to the pan.

6) Add 1 cup of water and salt to taste.

7) Cook for 3 to 4 minutes.

8) Turn off the hob and garnish with dry fenugreek leaves and chopped coriander leaves.

9) Serve hot with haryali pooris (page 187) or Coriander and garlic naan (page 189) and Masala Mushroom Fried Rice (page 173) or Vegetable Wild and Basmati Pilau (page 167).

Chicken Curry with a Hint of Spinach

This is Dalvi's simple but enticing chicken curry recipe. How can I forget my first cookery lesson on meat with my mother-in-law? Initially, my parents did not approve of our marriage which was upsetting, and they did not make it on our wedding day which was just painful. This gave birth to an amazing bond with my mother-in-law who promptly, knowingly/unknowingly filled the gap more than my mother would have.

In a way, it was a blessing in disguise, and I was always like a daughter to her. Like many other Indian households, food has always been a hot topic of discussion in Krish's family too. We used to talk about it all the time because a lot of dishes take hours to cook and prepare. We cooked a lot of Maharashtrian and North Indian dishes together when I was living with my in-laws. Being brought up in Mumbai, I was working on my *Marathi* (Krish's mother tongue) but the bond was getting stronger through our communication by exploring the family's guarded recipes and delicious food which nurtured and treasured my relationship with *Aai* ('Mum' in Marathi).

She was another beautiful soul, who believed in me and never gave up on me when I told her about leaving my well-paid teaching profession to follow my dream. She was incredibly supportive when we were getting my dream restaurant ready during the world pandemic. She always wanted to visit Dalvi's restaurant, but Covid-19 had its plans and took her far away from us.

If you have never cooked Indian meat curries before, I would advise that you start with this easy recipe, and yes, it does not take a long time either.

> Tip: You can make this curry dairy-free by substituting the yoghurt with coconut milk or lemon juice.

Ingredients (2 people)

(For marinade)

250 g chicken breast fillets or chicken thighs, diced

2 tbsp natural or Greek yoghurt

3 garlic cloves, grated, or ¼ tsp garlic purée

1 inch ginger, grated, or ½ tsp ginger purée

½ tsp turmeric powder

Salt to taste

(For cooking)

3 tbsp cooking oil

½ tsp cumin seeds

1 bay leaf

½ inch of cinnamon stick

1 -2 whole red chillies (optional)

¾ tsp garam masala

1½ tsp coriander powder

¼ tsp turmeric powder

¼ to 2 tsp chilli powder (it depends how spicy you would like your dish to be)

¼ tsp Dalvi's Magic Masala* (optional)

1 medium size onion, finely chopped

2 small tomatoes, finely chopped

Handful spinach, chopped

Salt to taste

1 tbsp coriander leaves, finely chopped

Instructions

1) Take a bowl and marinate the diced chicken in all the ingredients under the 'For marinade' heading for half an hour to 2 hours, or preferably overnight.

2) Heat the oil in a frying pan and when the oil is hot, add cinnamon stick, bay leaf and cumin seeds. Add whole red chillies if you like it spicy.

3) When cumin seeds start releasing their aromas, add onions, stir and cook the onions until the onions turn translucent (about 8–10 minutes).

4) Add chopped tomatoes, mix well with onions and add garam masala, coriander powder, turmeric powder, chilli powder and a bit of salt.

5) Mix everything, add a sprinkle of water and cover the pan and let it cook until oil separates or for 2–3 minutes.

6) Add diced chicken and mix everything. Add a splash of water.

7) Cover the frying pan and simmer until the chicken pieces are no longer pink in the centre and the juice runs clear for about 20 minutes. If it is necessary, add some more water. (This depends on what consistency you would prefer.)

8) Add chopped spinach and Dalvi's Magic Masala and mix it with chicken. Cook for a further 2 minutes.

9) Add chopped coriander leaves.

10) Serve with Naan or chapatis or rice.

* Available to buy from Dalvi's restaurant.

Dhaba Chicken

Dhaba means roadside restaurant. They are immensely popular in India and are established near highways. *Dhabas* are small mud shacks, usually found near fuel stations. Back in the day, these *dhabas* were busy catering to truck drivers who used to look for food that reminded them of home.

A few years ago, these mud shacks would have been run and operated by Punjabis or North Indians. But today eating at *Dhaba* in urban cities is a trend. Chicken sautéed in onion, tomato masala and flavoured with aromatic spices and served with Indian chapatis or parathas, *Dhaba* chicken is the perfect dish to indulge your chicken curry cravings. Growing up in Mumbai, the highlight of any road trip was a stopover at *dhaba* for steaming hot, spicy *dhaba*-style chicken with some rice and naan.

Ingredients (4 people)

(For marinade)

500 g of chicken, diced

4 tbsp Greek yoghurt

5 to 6 garlic cloves, grated

1½ inches of ginger, peeled and grated

1/4 tsp turmeric powder

½ tsp lemon juice

Salt to taste

(For cooking)

4 to 5 tbsp cooking oil

½ tsp cumin seeds

¼ tsp carom seeds (optional)

2 small bay leaves

2 inches cinnamon stick

1 black cardamom

1 ¼ tsp garam masala

3 tsp coriander powder

1 tsp cumin powder

½ tsp turmeric powder

¼ tsp to 2 tsp chilli powder (depends on how spicy you like your curry to be)

3 to 4 garlic cloves, finely chopped

½ inch ginger, finely chopped

4 medium onions, thinly sliced

2 small tomatoes, grated

3 tbsp gram flour or besan

Salt to taste

1 tsp dry fenugreek leaves or *kasuri methi* (optional)

2 tbsp fresh coriander, finely chopped

Instructions

1) Take a bowl and marinate the chicken with all the other ingredients under the 'For marinade' heading. Marinade this chicken for 30 minutes to 2 hours in the fridge.

2) Heat the oil in a pan on a medium heat. When the oil is hot, add cinnamon stick, bay leaf, black cardamom, carom seeds and cumin seeds.

3) When cumin seeds start releasing aroma add finely chopped ginger and garlic. Sauté for around 30 seconds.

4) Once the raw smell of garlic is gone, add thinly sliced onions. Cook onions until they are light brown (approximately 10–12 minutes).

5) Heat another pan on a low heat and add gram flour. Dry-roast the flour for 3 to 4 minutes, always stirring. Turn the hob off and put it aside to cool down.

6) Check the onions and now add grated tomatoes, chilli powder, turmeric powder, cumin powder, garam masala and salt. Mix everything well. Add a splash of water.

7) Put the lid on and let the mixture cook until the oil starts separating.

8) Add marinated chicken and roasted gram flour and mix everything well.

9) Now add 100 ml of water. Mix everything. Cover the pan and let the chicken cook for 20 -25 minutes on a low heat.

10) Keep checking. If necessary, add a splash of water.

11) Add Dalvi's Magic Masala and mix everything well. Cook for a further 2 minutes.

12) Turn off the hob and add chopped coriander leaves.

13) Serve with naan, pooris or rice of your choice.

Butter Chicken

Butter chicken – a heart-warming dish.*

Butter chicken is a dish where marinated tender chicken breast or thigh is cooked in a mixture of aromatic spices, herbs, cream of onion and tomato and cashews. My daughter (Aarya) says, "Every bite of butter chicken with parathas and rice takes you to heaven."

Butter chicken, as many know, was invented during the partition years of India and Pakistan by Kundan Lal Gujral. As I mentioned before, I wasn't allowed to eat any meat when living with my parents. I used to fulfil my desire of enjoying this curry by going to a Punjabi restaurant near my university. I must say, so-called *murgh makhani* (butter chicken) was my favourite; it was an absolute joy to eat such a treat when your family forbids you! After eating butter chicken in India, I was desperate to find the same taste, texture and flavours here in the UK. Sadly, I couldn't find that real butter chicken. Frustratingly, the butter chicken used to be either too sweet or overly creamy, leaving you bloated.

The recipe I am sharing is simple. I am sure you will enjoy every bite of your homemade butter chicken, and you will not feel bloated afterwards.

> **TIP:** You can add paneer if you want to make it vegetarian. Just add shallow-fried chopped pepper cubes and onions with paneer. And that will give you Kadahi paneer.

* https://www.indianweekender.co.nz/Pages/ArticleDetails/99/16736/recipes/when-butter-met-chicken-a-mouthwatering-love-story

Ingredients (4 people)

(For marinade)

500 g boneless chicken, diced

8 tbsp Greek or plain or natural yoghurt

5–6 garlic cloves, grated, or 1 tsp garlic purée

2 inches of ginger, grated, or 1 tsp ginger paste

¼ tsp turmeric powder

Salt to taste

(For first cooking)

4 tbsp cooking oil

2 pinches of asafoetida

2 medium onions, roughly chopped

3 small tomatoes, roughly chopped

3 to 4 garlic cloves

1 inch ginger, roughly chopped

¼ tsp cumin seeds

1 inch cinnamon stick

4 to 5 black peppercorns

1 to 3 dry red chillies (as per your taste)

handful cashews

(For second cooking)

2 tbsp oil and 25 g of butter

½ cup or 65 g double cream (optional)

2 small bay leaves

½ tsp turmeric powder

¼ tsp to 2 tsp chilli powder (depends how spicy you would like your curry to be)

2 tsp garam masala

4 tsp coriander powder

1 tbsp coriander leaves, finely chopped

1 tbsp dry fenugreek leaves (*kasuri methi*)

¼ tsp Dalvi's Magic Masala* (optional)

Salt to taste

TIP: If you are allergic to nuts and dairy, you can always avoid the use of nuts and dairy for this recipe.

* Available to buy from Dalvi's restaurant.

MAGICAL MUMBAI FLAVOURS

Instructions

1) Take a bowl and mix all the ingredients under the 'For marinade' heading. Cover the bowl and keep this marinated chicken for 30 minutes to 2 hours (preferably overnight) in the fridge.

2) Heat 4 tablespoons of oil in a pan on a medium heat. When oil is hot, add cumin seeds, asafoetida, black peppercorns, red chillies and cinnamon stick.

3) When cumin seeds start releasing aroma, add chopped garlic and ginger and cook until the raw smell of garlic goes away.

4) Now add chopped onions. Cook for 7 to 8 minutes on a medium heat. Add chopped tomatoes and mix everything.

5) Let this mixture cook for a further 3 to 4 minutes on a low heat. Add cashews and mix everything together and cook for 2 minutes.

6) Turn off the hob, keep the mixture aside and let everything cool down. Once everything has cooled down, blend the mixture to a fine purée.

7) Take another pan. Heat 2 tbsp oil and 25 g butter on a medium heat. When butter is melted, add 2 small bay leaves.

8) Turn the hob to a low heat and add turmeric and chilli powder and mix everything well.

9) Now add marinated chicken and ¼ cup of water. Mix everything together and let the chicken cook for 10 to 12 minutes.

10) Add blended purée to chicken. Add garam masala, coriander powder and double cream. Mix everything together and, if necessary, add a splash of water.

11) Let the chicken cook for a further 5 to 8 minutes until chicken is cooked thoroughly.

12) Now add Dalvi's Magic Masala, dry fenugreek leaves and chopped coriander.

13) Serve hot with naan bread and rice of your choice.

Butter Chicken Pizza

This is an all-time favourite pizza in the Dalvi household and at Dalvi's restaurant. This pizza works for any fussy eaters out there. You can add as many or as few toppings as you like.

> **TIP:** If you are vegetarian you can replace chicken with paneer or blanched cauliflower and broccoli florets.

Ingredients

500 g all-purpose flour or plain flour

7 g instant yeast or active dry yeast

300ml warm water (between 100 and 106°C)

½ tbsp sugar (for activating yeast)

½ tsp oregano

¼ tsp garlic powder

¾ tsp salt

120ml passata or tomato purée

1 cup butter chicken with 18–20 pieces of chicken

200 g mozzarella cheese balls, sliced

200 g mozzarella grated cheese

1 cup mixed peppers, cubed

1 small red onion, cubed

4 tbsp semolina

1 tbsp olive oil or any cooking oil

Instructions

1) Take a bowl, add warm water, sugar and dry yeast and give it a quick stir. Cover this bowl and put this away for 5 to 7 minutes. (You need to wait until little bubbles are formed.)

2) Once your yeast is frothy and bubbly, add all-purpose flour or plain flour. Add salt, sugar, oregano and garlic powder.

3) You can make a dough either with the help of an electric mixer or with your hands.

4) If you think your dough is a bit wet, add some flour. If your dough feels a bit dry, add a tiny bit of water. Make it into a ball.

5) Take a bowl and spread olive oil and sprinkle semolina in that bowl. Place your dough and grease it with some oil so that it doesn't get dry. Cover the bowl with a damp cloth.

6) Place the dough in a warm place for at least two hours, until the dough has doubled in size.

7) Get the dough out and punch down the risen dough to release air bubbles.

8) Divide the dough into two parts.

9) Roll each smaller dough out into a 12-inch circle.

10) Take a pizza tray and grease with some oil. Spread your rolled pizza on this tray. Brush some oil on the top to prevent the filling from making your pizza crust soggy.

11) Pre-heat the oven at 170°C for 15 minutes.

12) Spread tomato purée and butter chicken sauce over the dough with the back of your spoon.

13) Add sliced mozzarella cheese balls and spread on your dough along with some grated mozzarella cheese. Cut your chicken pieces into smaller pieces from the curry. Add them to pizza with mixed peppers and red onion cubes. Add some more grated mozzarella cheese on the top.

14) Bake for 12- 15 minutes at 180°C or until the cheese has melted and the crust is crisp and browned.

TIP: Check whether your dough is done by pressing the dough with your finger. It must bounce back. Your dough must be clean and bouncy.

Malwani (Malvani) Chicken

Malwani Chicken, or *Chicken Sagoti*, is cooked with a unique mixture of coconut and onions called watap. This magical chemistry of flavours was kept hidden from me until I found the love of my life. After a rebellious inter-caste marriage, I was introduced to Malwani cuisine by Krish's family, and I fell in love with this treasured, flavoursome chicken recipe. This truly scrumptious Maharashtrian dish has already created its mark along the Wyre and Fylde coast in Lancashire, United Kingdom. And I am sure it is going to be your family favourite too.

My mouth starts drooling even thinking about the first unforgettable taste of this curry with a special poori called vade (made with a mixture of rice, different kinds of lentils and whole spices). That was the first time I tried this exquisite Malvani dish. Historically, Malvan is one of the coastal towns in the Sindhudurg district of Maharashtra. It is very famous for its clean beaches and mouth-watering seafood and meat dishes. Malwani cuisine uses coconut in various forms – from grated coconut to coconut water.

Ingredients (4 people)

(For marinade)

500 g chicken

5 to 6 garlic cloves, grated, or 1 tsp garlic paste

2 inch of ginger, grated, or 1 tsp ginger paste

6 tbsp yoghurt

Salt to taste

¼ tsp turmeric

(For watap (onion and coconut paste))

½ cup desiccated coconut

1 small onion, roughly chopped

¼ tsp cumin seeds

¼ tsp coriander seeds

1 to 2 dry red chillies

4 to 5 black peppercorns

3 to 4 garlic cloves

½ inch ginger

2 tbsp cooking oil

(For second cooking)

3 tbsp cooking oil

1 inch cinnamon stick

1 bay leaf

2 medium onions, finely chopped

1 tomato, finely chopped

½ tsp turmeric

1 tsp garam masala

2 tsp coriander powder

¼ tsp to 2 tsp chilli powder

Salt to taste

1 tbsp fresh coriander leaves, finely chopped

Instructions

1) Take a bowl and marinate chicken with all the other ingredients under the 'For marinade' heading. Cover with cling film and put the bowl in the fridge for 30 minutes to an hour.

2) Heat 2 tbsp oil on a medium heat. When oil is hot, add roughly chopped onions, garlic and ginger and the whole spices under the 'For watap' heading.

3) Sauté and cook for 10–15 minutes until onions are light brown. Transfer this mixture to a bowl.

4) In the same pan, roast desiccated coconut on a low heat. Sauté for 3 to 4 minutes. When desiccated coconut looks light brown, transfer this to the same bowl of onion garlic and other whole spices. Let the mixture cool down. Now, grind the mixture to a smooth paste and put it aside. (Add water gradually when grinding to make watap.)

5) Heat 3 tbsp oil in *kadahi* or deep base pan on a medium heat. When oil is hot, add cinnamon stick and bay leaves. Sauté for 20 seconds or so and then add finely chopped onions.

6) Sauté and cook onions for 10–15 minutes or until onions are golden brown.

7) Add finely chopped tomatoes and all the dry spices under the 'For second cooking' heading. Add ¼ cup of water and mix everything well. Put the lid on and let the mixture cook for 4 to 5 minutes or until oil starts separating.

8) Now add diced chicken, ground watap and salt. Mix everything together. Now add ¼ cup of water and mix.

9) Put the lid on and cook for 15–20 minutes or until the chicken is cooked on a low to medium heat. Keep checking and, if necessary, add some water.

10) Turn the hob off. Add finely chopped coriander leaves.

11) Serve hot with chapati or naan and choice of your rice.

Malai Kadahi Chicken

Malai Kadahi chicken is a North Indian-style curry with creamy, flavoursome onion gravy that will have you finishing every single bite. If you are a vegetarian you can replace the chicken with paneer or parboiled vegetables like cauliflower or broccoli.

Serve it will masala laccha paratha (page 195) or naan and rice of your choice.

Ingredients (4 people)

(For cashew paste)

Handful cashews

1 tbsp poppy seeds

1 tbsp sesame seeds (optional)

(For onion paste)

1 onion, chopped

1 inch ginger

1–2 green chillies

1–2 garlic cloves

(For marinade)

500 g of chicken thigh or breast, diced

2 inches ginger, peeled and grated, or 1 tsp ginger paste

3 to 5 garlic cloves, grated, or 1 tsp garlic paste

½ cup double cream or heavy cream

Salt to taste

¼ tsp black pepper, ground

1 tsp cumin powder

¼ tsp white pepper powder (optional)

½ lemon

(For cooking)

1 small onion, chopped into cubes

1 green or red pepper, chopped into squares

1-2 green chillies (finely chopped) (optional)

3 -4 tbsp cooking oil

2 tbsp butter

½ tsp cumin seeds

¼ tsp black pepper, ground

2 tsp garam masala

4 tsp coriander powder

½ tsp chilli powder (optional)

1 tsp fenugreek leaves

½ cup whisked yoghurt

Salt to taste

1 tbsp coriander, finely chopped

Instructions

1) Take a bowl and marinate chicken with ingredients mentioned under 'For marinade' and keep the bowl in the fridge for an hour.

2) Take a small bowl and soak cashew nuts, sesame seeds and poppy seeds in 100 ml hot water for 30 minutes, and after 30 minutes grind this mixture to a smooth paste

3) Heat 2 tbsp oil in a pan on a medium heat. Add chopped onion cubes and square chopped green or red peppers. Fry them for 3–4 minutes. Turn the heat off and put this pan to one side.

4) **Onion Paste:** Take a grinder and add chopped onions, ginger, garlic and chillies. Add a splash of water and grind them to a smooth purée.

5) Heat 2 tbsp oil in a pan on a medium heat. Add marinated chicken and cook for 10–15 minutes until chicken pieces are cooked through. Move them into a bowl.

6) Now, in the same pan, add 2 tbsp oil and butter. When the butter starts melting, add cumin seeds. Sauté for a few seconds. When cumin seeds start releasing aroma, add onion paste you made at stage 4 and cook for 10–15 minutes until they change colour and become a bit brown.

7) Add whisked yoghurt and mix well.

8) Add finely chopped green chillies. Sauté for 20 seconds.

9) Add garam masala, ground black pepper, coriander powder, chilli powder, salt to taste and mix everything well.

10) Add fried onion, pepper and cooked chicken from step 3 and step 5. Mix everything well.

11) Now add ½ cup water and mix with chicken, onion and pepper.

12) Add blended cashew paste, cream, fenugreek leaves and coriander leaves.

13) Cook for 2 minutes or so and turn off the hob.

14) Serve with rice of your choice and naan.

Kerala-Style Lamb Curry

This staple food of Kerala swirls around an abundance of ingredients like coconut, black pepper, cloves, cardamom, cinnamon, curry leaves, etc. Kerala cuisine is well known for its unique flavours, simplicity and delectable food.

If you are in Mumbai or other parts of India, many people like cooking their meat in a pressure cooker. I always like the slow-cooked method – yes, it takes a bit longer, but the taste is always divine. I invariably cook lamb or goat meat on a low flame to retain its tenderness and moisture, and the spices get soaked in well.

Kerala cuisine is one of my favourites. I always crave to sample every time I am in Mumbai and since 2018 me and my family always make sure that we visit Kerala Lunch Home in Goregoan. I have tasted this curry with goat meat when I was in my teens. I know it can be tricky with lamb, but I can assure you that after marination, the aroma from the spices will successively eliminate the raw odour of the meat, and your cooked lamb will be deliciously infused with flavours.

TIP: You can use chicken or prawns if you are not a fan of lamb.

Ingredients (for 4 people)

(For marinade)

¼ tsp red chilli powder

¼ tsp salt

½ lemon juice

¼ tsp garam masala

2 pinches of black pepper, ground

500 g lamb, diced

(Spices to roast and grind)

1 tbsp coriander seeds

½ tsp fennel seeds

½ tsp cumin seeds

4 to 5 whole cloves

3 green cardamom

2 to 4 dry red chillies (optional)

½ inch of cinnamon stick

5 to 6 black peppercorn

(For cooking)

3 -4 tbsp coconut oil

3 medium size onions, finely chopped

1 tsp ginger paste or 2 inches of ginger, grated

1 tsp garlic paste or 3–5 garlic cloves, grated

1 cup or 230ml coconut milk

2 small tomatoes, finely chopped

½ tsp turmeric powder

¼ tsp to 2 tsp chilli powder (depends on how spicy you would like your curry to be)

(For tempering)

2 tbsp coconut oil

1 to 2 red chillies (optional) (break them and remove the seeds)

1 shallot, thinly sliced

¼ tsp mustard seeds

5 to 8 curry leaves (optional)

Instructions

1) Marinate lamb in all the ingredients mentioned under 'For marinade'. Keep marinated lamb in the fridge for 30 minutes to an hour.

2) Heat a pan on a medium heat. When the pan is hot, turn the hob down to low heat and add cumin seeds, cardamom pods, cinnamon stick, cloves, coriander seeds, dry red chillies, fennel seeds and black pepper. (mentioned in spices to roast and grind)

3) Stir the spices until they begin to go light brown and release their aromas. Turn the heat off.

4) Let the mixture cool down and transfer spices with a pinch of salt to a clean and dry spice grinder and grind to a coarse powder. Or you can use a mortar and pestle.

5) Heat coconut oil in a pan on a medium heat. Add finely chopped onions and fry them until they turn gold, around 12 to 15 minutes.

6) Add grated ginger and garlic. Fry until the raw smell goes away.

7) Add marinated lamb or chicken and fry on a medium to high heat for 3 to 4 minutes.

8) Now add the ground spices, turmeric powder and chilli powder and mix well. Cook for 2 minutes.

9) Now add tomatoes and mix everything well.

10) Put the lid on and cook on a low heat for 40 to 45 minutes or until lamb is cooked.

11) Keep stirring every few minutes and if, necessary add splash of water.

12) Add coconut milk and when coconut milk begins to bubble cover and simmer for 5 minutes. Check salt and adjust as needed. Turn off the hob.

13) Now, heat a small pan with coconut oil on a medium heat. When oil is hot, add mustard seeds. When they start releasing aroma, add and fry thinly sliced shallots until they turn pink.

14) Add curry leaves and red chillies.

15) Turn the hob off when leaves turn crisp.

16) Pour this over the curry.

17) Serve this curry with rice, chapati or paratha.

> **TIP:** If you are using prawns, please add prawns after stage 9 and cook for 10 minutes or until prawns are cooked.

Mangshor Jhol Lamb

This is a Bengali-style curry where lamb pieces are cooked with large-sized potatoes in a *jhol*, a soup-like gravy. So, the curry should be thinner in consistency than usual. I remember cooking this curry with my much-loved sister-in-law. My husband's family are very used to eating Maharashtrian-style food, so it was tricky to meet the expectation with this too. The recipe differs from family to family, and I am sharing the recipe which I used with my sister-in-law. Now it's a must-have curry when I visit my in-laws in Mumbai.

Ingredients (4 people)

(For marinade)

500 g of lamb, diced (with or without bone)

1 medium onion (grated)

3 to 5 garlic, grated, or 1 tsp garlic paste

2 inches of ginger, grated, or 1 tsp ginger paste

¼ tsp turmeric powder

1 tbsp white vinegar

1 tbsp cooking oil (preferably mustard oil)

¼ tsp salt

(Other ingredients)

2 medium potatoes, peeled and cut into halves

3 medium onions, finely chopped

¼ tsp black pepper, ground

2 to 3 garlic cloves, grated

½ inch ginger, grated

1½ tsp coriander powder

¼ tsp turmeric powder

¼ tsp to 2 tsp red chilli powder (as per the spice level you prefer)

¾ tsp garam masala

4 tbsp natural yoghurt

½ tsp sugar

½ cup cooking oil (preferably mustard oil)

Salt to taste

(For tempering)

25 g butter or 4 tsp ghee

1 tbsp cooking oil (preferably mustard oil)

1 small bay leaf

1 to 2 dry red chillies

1 black cardamom

2 to 3 green cardamom

4 whole cloves

½ inch cinnamon stick

¼ tsp cumin seeds

Instructions

1) Take a bowl and marinate lamb pieces with all the ingredients mentioned under 'For marinade'. Mix everything well. Cover and keep the meat with the marinade in the fridge for at least 2 hours, preferably overnight.

2) Smear little salt and turmeric powder and ground black pepper onto the peeled and halved potatoes. Heat ½ cup oil in pan or *kadahi* or wok. Fry the potato pieces till golden brown. Take them out of the pan and keep them aside.

3) Now in the same pan, add butter or ghee to the oil. Temper the ghee and oil with all the ingredients mentioned under 'For tempering'.

4) When the whole spices start releasing aromas, add ½ cup cooking oil and then add finely chopped onions and cook them on a medium heat until the onion turns soft.

5) Now add sugar. Cook for a further 2 minutes.

6) Add the grated ginger and garlic and cook for a minute or so.

7) Now add marinated lamb pieces with all the marinade. Mix everything well and sauté the meat for another 5 minutes on a medium to high heat.

8) Add 4 tbsp yoghurt and salt. Mix everything well and keep stirring for 3 to 4 minutes on a medium heat.

9) Now add turmeric, chilli powder, coriander powder and garam masala. Mix everything well. Stir continuously until the oil starts separating from the sides of the pan/*kadahi*.

10) Now add 1 cup of boiled water. Mix everything well. Cook on a low heat for 25 to 35 minutes or until lamb is cooked through.

11) Now add fried potatoes, mix with curry and cook for a further 5 minutes.

12) Serve hot with steamed rice and chapati.

TIP: You can replace lamb with chicken or fish like red snapper.

Minced Lamb Kofta Curry

Koftas or *kofte* are very common in world cuisine. They are sophisticated delicacies, varying in taste and texture, depending on the country and regions they hail from.

This kofta curry is much-loved in the Dalvi household, where it is a show-stopper. It's a traditional Mughlai curry that is popular not only in Hyderabad but all over the world. Koftas are small balls made from either minced meat or fish or vegetables or lentils and cooked in a sea of onion and a creamy tomato purée, yoghurt, aromatic spices and herbs. During the zenith of the British Raj, a whole new genre of cooking evolved in India and this kofta curry arrived in India from Persia.

This is more than just a meatball curry.

You can use minced lamb, beef or goat meat for this recipe. This curry is for the dinner party menu and will leave your guests wanting more.

Ingredients (3 people)

(For kofta ball marinade)

300 g of minced lamb

3 to 4 garlic cloves, grated

1 inch ginger, grated

1 tbsp coriander leaves, finely chopped

1 tbsp fresh mint leaves, finely chopped

¼ tsp turmeric powder

¼ tsp cumin powder

3 tbsp breadcrumbs

1 egg, beaten

1 to 3 green chillies, finely chopped

2 cups of oil for deep-frying koftas

(For curry)

3 to 4 tbsp cooking oil

2 medium onions, puréed

3 to 4 garlic cloves, finely chopped

1 inch ginger, finely chopped

2 medium tomatoes, puréed

½ tsp turmeric powder

¼ tsp cumin powder

¾ tsp garam masala

1½ tsp coriander powder

¼ cup of cashews, blended to a paste

½ cup of double cream

1 tbsp kasuri methi (dry fenugreek leaves)

1 tbsp fresh coriander leaves, finely chopped

Salt to taste

Instructions

1) Take a bowl and mix all the ingredients mentioned under 'For kofta marination'.

2) Make small kofta balls (the size of a small lime). Put them on a baking sheet, cover them with cling film and put them in the fridge for 1 to 2 hours.

3) Take a pan or *kadahi* and heat 2 cups of oil on a medium heat. When the oil is hot, fry the kofta balls until the meat is cooked on a low medium heat (roughly 7 to 9 minutes).

4) Fry all the koftas and put them aside.

5) Now take another pan and add 3 to 4 tbsp oil. Heat the oil on a medium heat and when oil is hot, add grated garlic and ginger. Sauté them for a few seconds.

6) When the raw smell of garlic is gone, add onion purée. Cook the purée for 5 to 6 minutes on a medium heat, stirring frequently.

7) Once the purée becomes golden brown, add tomato purée, cumin powder, turmeric, coriander powder, chilli powder and two tbsp water. Mix everything well. Put the lid on and let this mixture cook for 3 to 4 minutes, until oil starts separating and it begins to thicken.

8) Now add blended cashew paste and cream to the sauce.

9) Mix everything together and if necessary, add a splash of water. Cook for a further 3 to 5 minutes.

10) Now add some water if necessary and fried koftas to curry.

11) Add garam masala and kasuri methi to the curry. Mix well.

12) Turn the heat to low, put the lid on and cook for 5 to 6 minutes.

13) Turn the hob off and add chopped coriander leaves.

14) Serve with naan and rice.

Prawn Masala

My mother-in-law says that milk and seafood are a bad combination for your body. According to *Ayurveda* (a healthy life system that people in India have used for more than 5000 years),* consuming milk with seafood increases vitiligo, a long-term condition where pale white patches develop on the skin. Science does not necessarily agree, and there are arguments about this. When I cook this curry, I always do it the way my mother-in-law used to do it. I use either lemon juice or coconut milk with this dish as these two ingredients go hand in hand with prawn dishes.

You can eat this curry either with rice or naan or chapatis. I love it with plain rice!

Ingredients (2 people)

(For marinade)

16 to 18 king prawns

1 tbsp lemon juice

2–3 garlic cloves, grated

½ inch ginger, grated

¼ tsp turmeric powder

Salt to taste

1 tbsp coconut milk

(For cooking)

3 tbsp cooking oil

¼ tsp cumin seeds

1 bay leaf

½ inch cinnamon stick

2 dry red chillies (optional)

½ tsp garam masala

1 tsp coriander powder

½ tsp turmeric powder

¼ tsp to 2 tsp chilli powder

100 ml coconut milk

¼ tsp Dalvi's Magic Masala** (optional)

2 small onions, finely chopped

1 small tomato, finely chopped

1–3 garlic cloves, grated, or ½ tsp garlic paste

½ inch ginger, grated

Salt to taste

1 tbsp coriander leaves, finely chopped

---

* https://m.timesofindia.com/life-style/food-news/fish-and-milk-toxic-combination-or-superstition/amp_articleshow/69280234.cms

** Available to buy from Dalvi's restaurant.

Instructions

1) Take a bowl and marinate all the prawns with all the ingredients mentioned under 'For marinade' for 15 minutes.

2) Heat the oil in a frying pan on a medium heat. Add cumin seeds, bay leaf and whole red or green chillies (If you like your curries to be spicy).

3) When cumin seeds start releasing aroma, add the onions, stir, and cook the onions until they turn translucent (about 7–8 minutes). Add grated ginger and garlic and cook for 30 seconds.

4) Add chopped tomatoes, mix well with onions and add garam masala, coriander powder, turmeric powder, chilli powder and a bit of salt.

5) Mix everything together, add coconut milk and cover the pan and let it cook for 30 seconds.

6) Add marinated prawns and mix everything together.

7) Cover the frying pan and simmer until all the prawns are cooked (about 8 to 10 minutes).

8) Add Dalvi's Magic Masala and mix it with prawns. Cook for a further 2 minutes on a low heat.

9) Turn off the hob, add chopped coriander leaves and let it settle for 10 minutes.

10) Serve with naan or chapatis or rice.

TIP: You don't have to marinate prawns for more than 15 minutes when you are using lemon or lime. If you marinate prawns in lemon for longer they start cooking in lemon acid.

Dalvi's Salmon Curry

Believe it or not, I started loving this fish when I came to live in the United Kingdom. I love fresh fish and now salmon is my all-time favourite. Salmon was the only fish I thought I could adapt a family recipe. After a few experiments, I have found what spices goes well with salmon curry. It is very popular not only in the Dalvi household but at Dalvi's restaurant too.

Ingredients (2 people)

(For marinade)

180 g of skinless salmon fillet

¼ tsp honey

¼ tsp black pepper

½ tsp lemon juice

2 garlic cloves, grated

½ inch of ginger, grated

1 tbsp olive oil

¼ tsp turmeric powder

2 pinches of rock salt

(For cooking)

1 small onion, finely chopped

1 small tomato, finely chopped

1 to 3 red or green chillies (optional)

½ inch ginger, finely chopped

1 to 2 garlic cloves, finely chopped

1 small bay leaf

1 inch cinnamon stick

¼ tsp fennel seeds

6–8 fenugreek seeds

¼ tsp onion seeds

¼ tsp coriander seeds

½ tsp Italian herbs

½ tsp turmeric powder

¼ tsp to 2 tsp chilli powder (depends on how spicy you would like your curry to be)

½ tsp garam masala

1 tbsp olive oil or any other cooking oil

¼ tsp Dalvi's Magic Masala* (optional)

1 tbsp fresh coriander leaves or parsley, finely chopped

---

* Available to buy from Dalvi's restaurant.

Instructions

1) Take a bowl and add all the ingredients under 'For marinade', apart from the salmon, and mix well. Now add salmon and gently massage with this mixture.

2) Heat the oil in a frying pan on a medium heat. When oil is hot, add cinnamon stick, bay leaf, cumin seeds, onion seeds, coriander seeds, funnel seeds and fenugreek seeds. Add green chillies if you want to make your curry spicy.

3) When all the seeds start releasing their aromas, add finely chopped ginger and garlic and stir for a minute until the row aroma of garlic goes away.

4) Add the onions, stir and cook until the onions turn translucent (about 8 minutes).

5) Add the chopped tomatoes and mix well. Add turmeric, chilli powder, garam masala, coriander powder, salt to taste and a splash of water.

6) Mix everything together and let the mixture cook for a further 3 to 4 minutes on a low heat.

7) Add the salmon fillet to the pan and put some mixture on top of it. Add 2 tbsp water. Put the lid on and let the salmon cook for 7 to 9 minutes on a low heat.

8) Keep checking and, if necessary, add little water (a tablespoon at a time).

9) When salmon is nearly cooked, add Dalvi's Magic Masala, Italian herbs and chopped coriander leaves. Mix everything well and gently.

Red Snapper Fish Saar

When I got married, my mother-in-law made a lovely curry called *surmai saar*. *Surmai* means kingfish and *saar* mean gravy. I started loving fish and seafood more after getting married to my husband, Krish. The way my in-laws used to cook fish and seafood was just unbelievable. And I used to eat as if I hadn't had anything to eat for a week or so – you can imagine how greedy I was when it came to fish.

After coming to the United Kingdom, it was difficult to buy fresh kingfish at times, around the area we live. So I tried the same recipe with red snapper fish, and the taste was just heavenly. And since then, it's one of the all-time favourite fish curries in the Dalvi household.

It is a truly mouth-watering, creamy fish curry with the goodness of coconut milk, onions, kokum and aromatic whole and ground spices.

Fish is a quick and a great lunch or dinner option as it is loaded with a lot of nutrients like omega-3, protein and vitamins. Apart from healthiness, this curry is full of delectable flavours in a truly luscious gravy.

Kokum or Garcinia Indica is native to the Western Coastal region, i.e. the Goa and Konkan regions. It's a small red fruit that becomes dark purple when fully ripened. It is usually sold as a dried, sticky rind and is dark purple/black. When added to curries, it gives a natural pinkish colour with a sweet and sour taste. Kokum is also known as grandma's cure to acidity.

I am sure your family, friends and loved ones will love this curry.

TIPS:
a) If you can't find red snapper, you can try mackerel or pomfret or prawns.
b) If you can't find kokum you can use a tiny amount of tamarind to add the tang.

Ingredients (3 to 4 people)

(For marinade)

400 g Red snapper fish fillets

¼ tsp ginger and garlic paste (or 1 inch ginger and 4 garlic cloves, grated)

½ tsp black pepper, ground

¼ tsp turmeric powder

Salt

(For coconut purée)

2–4 garlic cloves, grated, or ½ tsp garlic paste

2 inches ginger, grated, or 1 tsp ginger paste

1–3 green chillies, chopped

1 cup fresh coconut, grated or finely chopped

¾ tsp turmeric powder

1 tsp garam masala

2 tsp coriander powder

¼ -1 tsp chilli powder (as per your choice)

(For cooking)

2 medium onions, finely chopped

3 to 4 kokum, soaked in 4 tbsp of warm water

¼ tsp cumin seeds

¼ tsp black onion seeds or kalonji

¼ tsp fennel seeds

6 to 7 fresh curry leaves

4–5 tbsp coconut oil or any cooking oil

200 ml coconut milk

2 tbsp fresh coriander, chopped

1 tbsp fresh mint leaves, chopped

Salt to taste

Instructions

1) Take a bowl and marinade fish with all the ingredients mentioned under 'For marinade'. Keep marinated fish aside for 10–15 minutes.

2) Take a food blender and grind fresh coconut with all the other spices, ginger and garlic mentioned under 'For coconut purée' with 2 cups of water to a fine paste. Add water gradually and not in one go.

3) Heat the oil in a pan on a medium heat. When the oil is hot, add cumin seeds, black onion seeds, fennel seeds and curry leaves. When seeds start releasing aromas, add chopped onions and ¼ tsp salt and cook onions for 8 to 10 minutes until onions are light brown.

4) Add coconut purée and cook until it boils.

5) Add marinated fish, put the lid on and cook on a low heat for 9 to 10 minutes.

6) Take the lid off and add soaked kokum with water and 100 ml of coconut water.

7) Cook for a further 2 minutes or until fish is cooked.

8) Take the lid off and add chopped coriander and mint. Mix everything gently so that you don't break fish.

9) Serve with any rice dish and pooris.

Rice Dishes

- *Lamb Biryani*
- *Chicken Ouzi with Curry Sauce and Raita*
- *Vegetable Wild and Basmati Pilau*
- *Chickpeas Pilau Rice*
- *Masala Mushroom Fried Rice*
- *Schezwan or Sichuan Fried Rice*
- *Pesto Fried Rice*
- *Upma*

Lamb Biryani

Just one word: 'heaven', or in Urdu: *Janat*!

This rice dish doesn't only look beautiful but tastes just magical.

In India, there are around 30 or maybe more different kinds of biryanis as it changes from region to region. Every biryani has its unique taste and cooking methods. Biryani is a rich and royal dish and used to be cooked for guests or on special occasions. But this trend is changing slowly now.

When working as a personal chef, this was the most often ordered biryani. I am excited to share this recipe with you. Succulent, juicy pieces of tender lamb are cooked in a mixture of selected herbs and spices and then layered with crisp onions, roasted nuts, aromatic basmati rice, freshly chopped coriander and mint.

> **TIPS:**
> a) marinade your lamb overnight to get that taste.
> b) If possible, use fresh ginger and garlic for cooking.
> c) mint leaves play an important part in this recipe.

Ingredients (4 people)

(For marinade)

500 g lamb, diced (with bone or boneless)

3 tbsp thick Greek yoghurt

1½ tsp garlic paste or 5–6 garlic cloves, grated

1 tsp ginger paste or 2-inch root ginger, grated

¼ tsp salt

(For cooking rice)

500 g basmati rice (washed and drained)

2 bay leaves

2 black cardamom pods

1 cinnamon stick

2 star anise flowers (optional)

2 tbsp cooking oil

½ tsp salt

1 litre water

(For cooking lamb)

4–5 tbsp cooking oil

2 tbsp ghee or 10 g of unsalted butter

½ tsp cumin seeds

½ tsp coriander seeds

2 medium onions, finely chopped

2 small tomatoes, chopped

4–5 garlic cloves, grated, or 1 tsp garlic paste

2 inches of ginger, grated, or 1 tsp ginger paste

1 to 4 birds-eye green chillies, finely chopped (as per your taste)

¼ tsp to 1½ tsp chilli powder (as per your spice level)

¾ tsp turmeric powder

2 tsp garam masala

4 tsp coriander powder

(For oven)

2 tbsp ghee or butter

2 tbsp fresh coriander leaves, finely chopped

1 tbsp fresh mint leaves, finely chopped

½ cup fried onion (see below for the recipe)

2 tbsp fried almond flakes (optional)

Handful cashews, fried

Handful pistachio, fried

2 generous pinches of saffron infused in 2 tbsp warm milk

Instructions

1) Take a bowl, add lamb and all the ingredients mentioned under 'For marinade'. Mix everything well. Keep the bowl in the fridge and leave to marinate for 2 hours or overnight.

2) Take a heavy-based pan with a lid and heat the cooking oil on a medium heat. When the oil is hot, add cumin seeds and coriander seeds. As the whole spices start releasing aroma, add grated ginger, garlic and chopped green chillies. Sauté them for a minute or so until the raw smell of garlic is gone.

3) Now add the chopped onions. Sauté the onions on a medium heat for 12–15 minutes until they are soft and turn light brown.

4) Now add turmeric, garam masala, coriander powder and chilli powder. Cook for a further 2 minutes.

5) Add the marinated meat and chopped tomatoes. Mix everything well. Now add ½ cup of water. Give it a stir, put the lid on and let the lamb cook for 35 to 45 minutes on a low heat. Give it a stir halfway through, making sure that the lamb is cooked and the masala has thickened. If necessary, do add a small quantity of water from time to time.

6) Heat 1 litre of water in a saucepan. Add all the ingredients mentioned under 'For cooking rice' but not the rice. Let this water boil on a high heat.

7) When the water is boiling, add the rice, stir and simmer for 10–15 minutes until the rice is 95% cooked. Drain the water and set aside.

8) For fried onions and nuts – thinly slice 2 medium white or brown onions into half-moons. In another pan, heat 4–5 tbsp cooking oil on a medium heat. Add thinly sliced onions and fry until deep golden brown (about 12–14 minutes). Make sure you keep on stirring. Now add cashews, pistachios and almond flakes. Stir and cook for a further 2 minutes. Turn off the hob and drain them on some paper towels.

9) Preheat the oven to 180°C fan (gas mark 4).

10) Brush the base of an over-proof deep pan (like a casserole) with some oil or melted butter or ghee. Cover a third of the base of the pan with a layer of cooked rice then the lamb with its sauce and then a layer of fried onions and nuts. Repeat the process, finishing off with a layer of rice and a drizzle of saffron milk, finely chopped coriander, mint leaves and 1 tablespoon of melted butter or ghee.

11) Cover the pan with tin foil or silver foil and a tight-fitting lid.

12) Place the dish in the middle of the oven for 10–12 minutes.

13) Serve with koshimbir raita (page 233), some chopped green chillies and onion rings.

Chicken Ouzi with Curry Sauce and Raita

Ouzi is a one-pot rice dish where chicken pilau is covered in filo pastry and cooked in an oven for a few minutes. This popular Middle Eastern dish is usually enjoyed during Ramadan.

I cannot describe how fabulous I thought ouzi was when I tried it for the first time. The inspiration for cooking this dish is a lovely lady called Sana who cooked lamb ouzi for me and my family when we stayed at my brother's house in Dubai for a few days.

For ouzi dishes, the filo pastry is used as a form of a carrier to carry cooked pilau instead of using a bag and container. Ouzi was traditionally a popular, on-the-go kind of food for poor people. Nowadays, this flavour-packed bag is used for weddings and other events just because ouzi looks tempting and tastes divine.

When I cook ouzi dishes, I always like marinating meat and cooking rice and meat with whole and ground spices. Instead of using filo pastry, I have used all-purpose flour dough. This chicken ouzi goes well with curry sauce and koshimbir raita (page 233).

Ingredients (4 people)

(For marinade)

500 g chicken, diced

3 tbsp Greek yoghurt or curd

1 tsp ginger garlic

1 tsp garlic paste

¼ tsp turmeric

¼ tsp ground black pepper

Salt to taste

(For dough)

Warm milk (as required)

2 tsp dry yeast or instant yeast

250 g all-purpose flour

½ tsp salt

200 ml warm water

3 tbsp yoghurt

Oil for greasing

(For cooking pilau)

300 g basmati rice (washed and drained)

2 onions, thinly chopped

1 tsp cumin seeds

¼ tsp asafoetida

2 bay leaf

1 star anise

2 inches cinnamon stick

2 black cardamom pods

1 tsp whole coriander seeds

1 tsp ginger garlic paste

1–4 green chillies, chopped (as per your taste)

½ tsp turmeric powder

3 tsp garam masala

5 tsp coriander powder

½ tsp chilli powder

½ cup plain yoghurt or curd

2 tbsp mint, chopped

½ cup oil

Salt to taste

(For curry sauce)

1 medium onion, finely chopped

2 tomatoes, puréed

2 garlic cloves, finely chopped

1 inch ginger, finely chopped

¼ tsp turmeric powder

½ tsp garam masala

1 tsp coriander powder

½ tsp chilli powder (optional)

Salt to taste

2–3 tbsp cooking oil

1 tbsp fresh coriander, finely chopped

Instructions

1) Take a bowl and marinate the chicken with all the ingredients mentioned under 'For marinade'.

2) Take a large bowl and add the all-purpose flour, sugar, salt, yeast, yoghurt and oil. Mix everything well.

3) Add warm water gradually and knead into a smooth dough. Grease this dough with 2 tbsp of oil and cover the bowl with cling film. Put the bowl in a warm place for 30 minutes or until the dough is double in size.

4) Heat the oil in a pan on a medium heat. When the oil is hot, add cinnamon stick, bay leaves, black cardamom pods, star anise, cumin seeds, coriander seeds and asafoetida.

5) When cumin seeds and coriander seeds start releasing their aroma, add chopped onions and sauté until slightly golden brown (around 20 minutes).

6) Add green chillies and ginger garlic paste. Cook until the raw smell of garlic disappears (for a minute or so).

7) Now add the marinated chicken and cook for 3 to 4 minutes.

8) Add turmeric powder, garam masala, coriander powder, chilli powder, yoghurt and mint. Mix everything together.

9) Add salt and ½ cup of water, put the lid on and cook for 4 to 5 minutes.

10) Now add 750 ml water and bring it to the boil.

11) Add rice to the pan and let it simmer until the water is reduced below the rice level.

12) Put the lid on and steam on a low heat for 12 to 15 minutes or until alll the water is gone and the rice is cooked and looks grainy. Now turn off the hob and your chicken pilau is ready.

13) For curry sauce – heat oil in a pan on a medium heat. When the oil is hot, add chopped ginger and garlic (or ginger and garlic paste). Sauté them for a minute or so until the raw smell of garlic goes away. Add chopped onions and sauté them for 10 to 15 minutes or so until they are light golden brown.

14) Add tomato purée, turmeric powder, garam masala, coriander powder, chilli powder and salt to taste. Add a splash of water and mix everything together. Let this mixture cook for 10 minutes or so on a low heat. Then add the finely chopped coriander and mix everything. Turn off the heat and put the curry sauce aside.

15) Pre-heat the oven for 10 minutes at 180°C fan (gas mark 4).

16) Take the dough previously put aside (see paragraphs 2 and 3 of 'Instructions') and roll it into a large disc-like shape (15cm diameter for an individual or 45cm diameter for 3 to 4 people).

17) Take a small bowl or a cereal bowl (if it is for one person) or take a big bowl (mixing bowl) if it is for a family and spread some oil around the surface. Place the rolled-out dough in a bowl, covering the sides of the bowl.

18) Fill in this bowl with the prepared chicken pilau. (Please make sure you don't fill this bowl to the very top.) Seal the top with the rest of the dough hanging outside the bowl. Brush the edges with milk to bind the dough together.

19) Flip the dough from the bowl into a baking tray, brush some milk over it and sprinkle some black onion seeds and chilli powder on top.

20) Bake in the pre-heated oven at 180°C (fan) for 15–20 minutes or until the outside dough is brown and crispy.

21) Serve with curry sauce and koshimbir raita (page 233).

Vegetable Wild and Basmati Pilau

Some dishes and their unique recipes leave a mark in your life as a milestone. Every time I try to master this particular dish to its perfection, it takes me back to the day when I was coming home with our first-ever bundle of joy, my daughter Aarya.

As a new mum, I never knew what to expect and was worried. On top of that, when you know you have a husband who can be overly creative with his culinary skills, you may end up ordering pizza to survive. On that day, I was anxious and worried when coming back home. The thought of looking after your baby, yourself and cooking can be very daunting!

But for me, my husband Krish was the best in looking after me as well as our baby daughter.

When we arrived home, the smell of freshly cooked vegetable wild and basmati pilau was welcoming and refreshing. I could see, sense and smell Krish's conception of healthy and tasty one-pot food on the table.

This one-pot rice dish is full of flavours, healthy and nutritious, and the best thing is, it doesn't take a lot of preparation.

Ingredients (2 people)

200 g wild and basmati rice

2 to 3 tbsp cooking oil

½ tsp cumin seeds

½ inch cinnamon stick

1 small bay leaf

4–6 broccoli florets

4–6 cauliflower florets

1 medium onion, finely chopped

65 g frozen peas

3 small baby corns, chopped in halves

1 small carrot, chopped

Handful spinach, roughly chopped

Handful cashews

1 tsp garam masala

Salt to taste

Instructionss

1) Rinse 200 g wild and basmati rice twice and soak this rice for 20 minutes. (Before adding rice to the pan, remember to drain the water.)

2) Meanwhile, take *a kadahi* or pan and heat the oil on a medium heat.

3) Add cumin seeds, cinnamon stick and bay leaf. Sauté them for a minute or so.

4) When cumin seeds start releasing aroma, add finely chopped onions. Sauté and cook them for 7 to 8 minutes. When onions turn golden brown, reduce the heat to low. Add broccoli, cauliflower, baby corn, chopped carrots, cashews, peas, rice, garam masala and salt. Mix everything together. Add 550 ml water.

5) Put the lid on and let everything cook for 10–15 minutes on a low heat or until the rice is cooked and all the water got absorbed.

6) Add chopped spinach and mix gently. Check whether the rice is cooked or not. If necessary, add a splash of water and cook for a further 2 minutes. Turn off the heat and put the lid back on and let it settle for a few minutes.

7) Enjoy this pilau with any curry or just with raita.

Chickpeas Pilau Rice

I am sure by now you all must have realised how my life has revolved around food with some remarkable and delicious memories. Isn't it just an awesome feeling how you associate a particular food recipe and unique taste with unforgettable events in your life that bring a contented smile to your face? My papa's special pilau recipe is close to my heart. My dad absolutely loves feeding people but he only steps into the kitchen on special occasions. We were lucky to enjoy Dad's cooking more or less every Saturday and now whenever we visit my mum and dad in Mumbai.

Whenever my dad used to go into the kitchen, he used to whip up a magical vegetarian dish. My mum would have a hard shift working with him as an assistant chef – chopping up vegetables, making ginger/garlic paste, reaching out for ingredients and cleaning up a hoard of mess left behind. But she always knew that it was worth a taste and nothing less but full of love.

Ingredients (2 people)

200 g basmati rice

150 g chickpeas, boiled or ready to eat

1 small onion, thinly chopped

2 to 3 tbsp cooking oil

¼ tsp cumin seeds

¼ tsp fennel seeds

¼ tsp coriander seeds

⅛ tsp fenugreek seeds

¼ tsp turmeric powder

½ tsp garam masala

1 tsp coriander powder

1/4 tsp chilli powder

Handful fresh coriander, finely chopped

Handful chopped spinach leaves (optional)

Instructions

1) Rinse the rice thoroughly in cold water until the water is clear. If you have time soak the rice in cold water for 20 minutes. This will help the grains cook more evenly.

2) Add 1 litre water to a saucepan and boil on a high heat. Add a tablespoon of oil and ¼ tsp oil.

3) Drain the water from the soaked rice. When the water in the pan is boiling, add rice, stir and let it cook on a medium heat for 10–12 minutes. You can tell when the rice is cooked by taking a grain between your forefinger and thumb and pressing down. It should still feel firm. Now drain the rice in a rice strainer.

4) Heat 2 tbsp oil in a pan on a medium heat. Once the oil is hot, add cumin seeds, coriander seeds, fennel seeds and fenugreek seeds and sauté for a few seconds.

5) When the seeds start releasing aroma, add thinly chopped onions and sauté for 10 to 15 minutes until the onion turns golden brown.

6) Now add all the ground spices, salt, chickpeas and cooked rice.

7) Mix everything together. Cook on a low heat for a further 2 minutes. (If you are using spinach this is the stage you add spinach to the pilau.)

8) Turn the hob off, add coriander leaves and mix everything together.

9) Serve hot with any curry or eat on its own with some yoghurt or raita.

Masala Mushroom Fried Rice

Mushrooms are full of nutrients and are very popular all over the world. However, things were different a few years back and mushrooms had very few takers in India. And the Sharma family (my maiden name) was one of them. When I was ten years old, one of our neighbours brought mushroom *sabzi* (curry) around and when she left, we weren't very sure about what to do with that curry because we had a lot of misgivings about mushrooms and had always believed that all mushrooms are magical. But the aroma of that curry or *sabzi* was suggesting a different belief. And so we ate that *sabzi* and since then, we all have fallen in love with mushrooms. And as time moved on, this mushroom *sabzi* or masala mushroom fried rice is a must-have dish when we visit India. Like the previous recipe, this too is especially cooked by my papa.

This mushroom fried rice is easy to cook and sumptuous if you are looking to treat your loved ones. Like my papa, I always use the left-over rice cooked a day before as it just gives the perfect taste and look. But you can cook fresh rice for this dish. I will leave that decision with you.

Ingredients (2 people)

200 g basmati rice

70–80 g white mushrooms, thinly sliced

2–3 tbsp cooking oil

1 small onion, finely chopped

½ tsp cumin seeds

2 garlic cloves, finely chopped

½ tsp dry Italian herbs

¼ tsp turmeric powder

2 pinches of black pepper, ground

¼ tsp to 1 tsp chilli powder

½ tsp lemon juice

1 tbsp fresh coriander or parsley, finely chopped

Salt to taste

Instructions

1) Rinse the rice thoroughly in cold water until water is clear. If you have time, soak the rice in cold water for 20 minutes. This will help the grains cook more evenly.

2) Add 1 litre water to a saucepan and boil on a high heat. Add a tablespoon of oil and ¼ tsp oil.

3) Drain the soaked rice. When the water in the pan is boiling, add rice, stir and let it cook on a low heat for 10 to 15 minutes or until rice is cooked.

4) Turn off the heat and drain the water from the rice. Put the rice aside.

5) Take a pan and heat the oil on a medium heat. When oil is hot, add cumin seeds and 2 pinches asafoetida. When cumin seeds start releasing aroma, add chopped garlic. Sauté for a minute or so. Add finely chopped onions. Sauté and cook onions for 7 to 8 minutes until onions turn golden brown.

6) Now turn the heat to low. Add turmeric, ground black pepper, chilli powder, lemon juice and salt.

7) Add thinly sliced mushrooms. Mix everything well. Put the lid on and cook mushrooms for 4 to 5 minutes on a low heat.

8) Now add cooked rice and Italian herbs and finely chopped coriander or parsley. Mix everything well. Cook for a further 2 minutes on a low heat. Turn the hob off.

9) Serve with any curry and enjoy!

Schezwan or Sichuan Fried Rice

Schezwan fried rice is a spicy Indo-Chinese fried rice made with Sichuan or Schezwan sauce. I remember enjoying this fried rice dish with Manchurian vegetables in my uni days – the good old days, when you could go to the restaurant, enjoy your favourite food and have a good time with your friends. As I discussed before, Indo-Chinese food is popular in India.

I love food fusion from different cuisine as it gives the best of both cuisines. And like a few more fusion recipes I have mentioned, this fiery dish is my all-time favourite since childhood. That Indian *tadka to* this Chinese dish is very much an Indian style because Chinese dishes are not spicy at all.

I am sure you will fall in love with this truly mouth-watering dish.

Ingredients (3 people)

300 g basmati rice

1 small onion, finely chopped

2–3 garlic cloves, finely chopped

½ inch of ginger, peeled and finely chopped

1 small carrot, julienne

2 tbsp French beans, chopped

1 small green pepper, julienne

½ cup of shredded white cabbage

1 tbsp Schezwan chutney (page 231)

¼ tsp black pepper, ground

1 tsp white vinegar

½ tsp soy sauce (optional)

2 tbsp rapeseed oil for stir-frying

1 tbsp spring onions chopped

½ tsp sesame seeds (optional)

Salt to taste

Instructions

1) Rinse the rice thoroughly in cold water until water is clear. If you have time, soak the rice in cold water for 20 minutes. This will help the grains cook more evenly.

2) Take a saucepan and add 1 litre water and boil it on high flame. Add a tablespoon of oil and ¼ tsp oil.

3) Drain the soaked rice. When water is boiling, add rice, stir and let it cook on a medium heat for 10 minutes. You can tell when the rice is cooked by taking a grain between your forefinger and thumb and pressing down. It should still feel firm. Now drain the rice in a rice strainer.

4) Heat the oil in a pan or wok on a medium heat. When the oil is hot, add garlic and ginger and sauté for a few seconds until the raw smell of garlic goes away.

5) Add the finely chopped onions to a pan. Stir-fry on a high heat for a minute or so.

6) Add all the vegetables and sauté them on a high heat for about 2 to 4 minutes, when the vegetables start to slightly brown.

7) You can cut down on the stir-frying time, if you prefer half-cooked or more crunchy vegetables.

8) Now reduce the heat to medium and add Schezwan chutney (page 231), salt, black pepper, vinegar and Soy sauce. Mix everything well.

9) Add rice and stir-fry on a high heat until the rice is coated with Schezwan chutney/sauce.

10) Add chopped spring onions to Schezwan rice and stir. Serve Schezwan rice hot in serving bowl or plate.

Pesto Fried Rice

Just two words – Truly awesome!

This dish goes well with chicken or lamb curry dishes. As I mentioned before, I love mixing two cultures. When you marry Indian spices with Italian cuisine you get a truly awesome dish like Pesto Fried Rice.

The credit for this dish goes to my children who love Italian food. It was created with leftover basmati rice, pesto sauce, some peppers, and spices. They loved it and now they always demand pesto fried rice at least once a week. I do hope that you enjoy this dish too.

I usually make pesto at home and freeze it in small containers.

Ingredients (3 people)

(For pesto sauce)

1 cup basil leaves

1 cup spinach leaves

½ cup freshly grated Parmesan (optional)

½ cup olive oil

½ cup pine nut or cashew nuts

8–10 black peppercorns

4 garlic cloves

Salt to taste

(For cooking)

3 cups cooked rice

2 tbsp olive oil

2 tbsp butter or ghee

1 small onion, chopped

1 cup mixed peppers, chopped

3 to 4 baby corns, chopped

½ tsp garam masala

½ tsp Italian mixed herbs

½ tsp dry oregano

2 tbsp fresh coriander, chopped

Salt to taste

Instructions

1) Take a blender and add spinach, blanched (see page 95), and all the other ingredients mentioned under 'For pesto'. If necessary, add some water and blend it to smooth purée.

2) Heat the oil and butter in a pan on a medium heat.

3) Add chopped onions and cook for 8–10 minutes until they are translucent.

4) Add chopped pepper and baby corn and sauté for 3 to 4 minutes. Add pesto sauce and cooked rice. Mix everything well. Sauté for 2 minutes or so on a low heat.

5) Add mixed herbs, dry oregano, garam masala and chopped coriander. Mix everything and cook for a minute or so.

6) Serve with any curry dishes or soup dishes.

Upma

Upma or uppumavu or uppittu originates from the South Indian states and is very common not only in those states but also in Maharashtra, Gujarat and also in Sri Lanka. The word *upma* in South Indian languages combines salt (uppu) and flour (pittu).

This gorgeous and healthy dish is cooked from semolina or *sooji*. There are many variations of upma in terms of the ingredients and spices used, depending on the region and one's preferences.

The recipe I am sharing here is from my sister-in-law (Wahini) and is a hit in the Dalvi household. Wahini is a fantastic cook when it comes to Maharashtrian cuisine.

A quick option for the weekends if you are fed up with eating cereal or bread toast or chapatis or parathas.

Ingredients (3 people)

175 g semolina

1 onion, chopped

1 to 4 bird's eye chillies, chopped (depends on your spice level)

1 inch root ginger, finely chopped

¼ tsp mustard seeds

¼ tsp cumin seeds

A pinch of hing (asafoetida)

4 to 5 curry leaves

2 tablespoon ghee (optional)

2 tbsp cooking oil

1 tsp salt (not heap; you can use less)

2 tsp sugar

¼ tsp garam masala

handful cashews

2 tbsp channa (gram) daal (I have used roasted gram)

1 tbsp fresh coriander leaves, finely chopped

625 ml water

Instructions

1) Heat a pan on a low heat. When the pan is hot, add ghee and semolina and roast. Keep stirring it until semolina gets light brown (5 to 6 minutes).

2) Empty the semolina into a dry bowl and put it aside.

3) On the same pan, heat the oil on a medium heat. Add mustard seeds, asafoetida and cumin seeds.

4) When these seeds start releasing aroma, add finely chopped ginger and green chillies. Add channa daal or roasted channa daal and cashews. Sauté them for a minute on a low heat.

5) Now add chopped onions. Sauté and cook onions for 6 to 7 minutes until they are translucent.

6) Add 625 ml of water, salt and sugar to a pan. Mix everything, put the lid on and boil the water on a medium heat. Please do keep an eye on this stage.

7) When the water is boiling, turn the heat down to low. Add roasted semolina and chopped coriander to the water. Mix everything well.

8) Put the lid on and let upma cook for 2 minutes.

9) Serve hot with either mint and coriander chutney or with any curry, or you can have it as a healthy breakfast.

Bread

- *Haryali Pooris*
- *Coriander and Garlic Naan*
- *Triangle Aloo Paneer Parathas*
- *Masala Laccha Paratha*

Haryali Pooris

Poori – puffed-up crispy bread loved by every Indian. Pooris are small, round, puffy fried bread made with wheat flour. Whatever the occasion, pooris are always the winner in Indian households. And I was the odd one out in my teenage. I just wasn't a fan of them, and I seriously don't understand why, because they are just delicious. As a child, I always found it mesmerising when a small piece of rolled-out dough used to puff up in the hot oil.

Haryali pooris are one step beyond normal pooris. These pooris are popular at Dalvi's restaurant, so I thought I would share this recipe with you all. If you don't want them to be green, you can make the dough without spinach. These pooris go well with any curry mentioned in this recipe book, or you can enjoy them on their own.

> **TIPS:**
> a) Adding *rava* (semolina) helps make your pooris crispier and helps keep your pooris puffed up for longer.
> b) Please make sure your dough is stiff and not soft like chapatis.
> c) Poori dough should never be rested for a long period.

Ingredients (2–4 people)

250 g wheat flour

50 g semolina (optional)

¼ tsp turmeric powder

¼ tsp garam masala

½ tsp coriander powder

¼ tsp chilli powder

120 ml water

Salt to taste

1 tbsp cooking oil for kneading and 500 ml oil for deep frying

1 cup spinach purée

Instructions

1) Mix the flour, semolina, turmeric, garam masala, coriander powder, chilli powder, 1 tbsp oil, spinach purée and salt to taste.

2) Mix everything well, coat flour with spinach purée and start kneading. Add water gradually if necessary and knead for 5 minutes or so until you have firm dough. (You might not use all the water.)

3) Pour a little oil into your hands and rub over the surface of the dough.

4) Wrap the dough in cling film and rest for 20 to 30 minutes.

5) Make small balls of the dough (half the size of a lime). Using dry wheat flour and a rolling pin, roll out 2mm thick round poori. Set aside while you roll out the rest. (Please don't stack rolled-out pooris on top of each other to prevent them sticking to each other.)

6) Now heat 500ml oil in a *kadahi* or heavy-based pan on a medium heat.

7) When the temperature of oil reaches 180°C, slip one rolled-out poori into the oil. When it comes to the surface, using a slotted spoon, lightly push it back under the oil until it puffs up and then turn it over and cook for 10 more seconds until golden brown.

8) Take the poori out and drain on the kitchen paper towel while you make the test.

9) Serve while it's still warm.

10) Enjoy pooris with any curry.

Coriander and Garlic Naan

If you are a fan of naan, you will love this simple recipe. These naans are easy to cook, and they taste amazing with any of the curries mentioned in the main curry chapter. These are no-yeast naans, and you can cook them on your kitchen hobs. This is how my nan would make them, and now me. The only difference is – my nan would cook them on an earthen stove that gave them crispy edges and an earthy aroma.

Ingredients (5–6 naans)

300 g all-purpose flour, plus extra flour for dusting and rolling

1 tsp sugar

1 tsp baking soda

100 g Greek yoghurt

2 tbsp cooking oil

1 tsp salt

30 ml warm water

90 ml warm milk

7 to 8 garlic cloves, grated

2 tbsp coriander, finely chopped

1 tbsp nigella seeds or *Kalonji*

30 g butter, oil or ghee

Instructions:

1) In a bowl, combine all-purpose flour, baking soda, salt and sugar.

2) Now add yoghurt, 1 tbsp oil and mix everything well.

3) Add water gradually and knead the flour to a soft dough. Be careful when adding water. If the dough is too dry add some water, but if the dough feels a little wet, add some extra flour.

4) Add some oil around the dough. Cover the dough with a damp tea towel and set aside in a warm place for at least 30 minutes.

5) Now divide the dough into 8 to 10 equal parts and roll each piece into a ball.

6) Take one ball and roll it out to 6- to 7-inch diameter with the help of some dry flour. Your naan doesn't have to be round.

7) Sprinkle some grated garlic, nigella seeds and coriander leaves and spread some melted butter or oil or ghee on it. Heat a large, heavy bottom pan or skillet over a high heat. Turn the heat down, add ½ tsp oil, ghee or butter and slap the garlic side down on the hot pan and lightly press.

8) When the bubbles begin to form on the surface (about a minute or so), flip the side. Press gently and cook until bubbles on this side are charred (about 1–2 minutes).

9) Sometimes I use tongs and once one side is cooked, I cook the other side on high flame with the help of tongs. (This is optional but if you feel confident, why not?!)

10) Brush naan with some more butter or ghee, then add some grated/chopped garlic and coriander.

Triangle Aloo (Potato) Paneer Parathas

Paratha, either plain or stuffed, with pickle or raita on the side, holds a huge place in Indians' hearts. Writing this recipe, I am so nostalgic with beautiful memories from the past, when Mum used to cook stuffed parathas for us for morning breakfasts.

A paratha is a wheat or all-purpose flour-based flatbread that has its origins in the Indian subcontinent. There are various types of stuffed parathas, but the one I am sharing with you is my all-time favourite – aloo paneer paratha. Parathas have been a popular breakfast in my household. And my mum is an expert in making a variety of parathas – simple layered paratha, aloo paratha, fenugreek leaves paratha and daal parathas, just to name a few.

Triangle aloo paneer paratha is wheat-based and stuffed with a delicious potato paneer filling. My mum, my nan and aunties always make round parathas. But I am sharing a recipe for triangles as I think making a triangle shape is easier and less messy.

Ingredients (7 to 8 parathas)

(For dough)

300 g chapati flour

50 g gram flour

¼ tsp carom seeds

Salt to taste

Some water

1 tbsp oil

(For stuffing)

2 boiled potatoes, grated

50 g paneer, grated

1 to 4 green chillies, finely chopped (as per your choice)

2–3 garlic cloves, grated, or ½ tsp garlic paste

1 tsp garam masala

2 tsp coriander powder

¼ tsp amchur powder or ½ a lemon

¼ tsp chilli powder

1 tbsp fresh coriander, finely chopped

Salt to taste

(For cooking)

Oil, ghee or butter as required

Instructions

1) Take a bowl and add chapati flour, gram flour, carom seeds and salt. Mix everything well.

2) Add water gradually and knead to a soft and pliable dough that does not stick to your fingers. If the dough is too dry add a little water at a time, until dough comes together nicely. Add 1 tsp oil and spread oil all over the dough.

3) Put the dough in a bowl and cover with cling film. Keep the dough at room temperature for 15 minutes.

4) Take a bowl and add grated potatoes, grated paneer, green chillies, garlic, garam masala, coriander powder, chopped coriander, amchur and salt. Mix everything well.

5) Take one small ball (lime-sized) from the dough. Dust it with some flour. With a rolling pin, roll the dough ball to a size of about 7 inches.

6) Now cut a single slice through the rolled dough from the outer edge to the centre.

7) Place potato and paneer filling in one quadrant (approximately 1.5 tbsp filling). Please leave some space around the edges of that quadrant.

8) Spread some oil or ghee on the remaining three quadrants.

9) Start folding the quadrant with potato filling and carefully fold each quarter over the other until you have a triangle-shaped chapati. Please do make sure the edges are stuck together firmly so that the filling doesn't come out.

10) Now spread some dry flour on the work surface and on the stuffed triangle and start rolling the triangle into a bigger triangle shape, very gently and lightly.

11) Heat a heavy-based pan or *roti tawa* on a medium heat.

12) Add 1 tsp oil, ghee or butter. Place the rolled paratha and cook until slightly brown. Flip the side and spread some oil on the top of the paratha. Cook for 30 seconds and flip and press the stuffed paratha edges with a spatula, so that they are fried well.

13) Once both sides are cooked, transfer them to a serving plate.

14) Cook all parathas in this way and stack them on a serving plate. Cover plate with silver foil.

15) Serve these parathas hot with raita, pickle or curry.

Masala Laccha Paratha

Laccha means layers and laccha paratha means a paratha that has layers. These parathas are immensely popular in North Indian cooking and are often eaten as breakfast with tea. But I always loved eating these parathas with homemade butter called *makhan*. In this recipe, I have made this layered paratha a bit *masaledar* (seasoned), as I am a big fan of spices and adding spices to these parathas take them to a next level.

These parathas taste yummy with any curries mentioned in the main curry chapter.

Ingredients (4 people)

300 g chapati flour	¼ tsp chilli powder
50 g gram flour	1 tbsp dry fenugreek leaves
¼ tsp salt	Some water
¼ tsp turmeric	1 tsp oil
½ garam masala	Organic ghee or butter (optional)

Instructions

1) Take a small bowl and add chilli powder, turmeric, fenugreek leaves and garam masala. Put this bowl aside as you will be using these spices once you have rolled chapati for paratha

2) Take a big bowl and add chapati flour, gram flour and salt. Mix everything together

3) Add water gradually and knead to a soft and pliable dough that does not stick to your fingers. If the dough is too dry add a little water at a time, until dough comes together nicely. Add 1 tsp oil and cover the dough with oil.

4) Put the dough in a bowl and cover this dough with cling film or a lid. Keep the dough at room temperature for 15 minutes.

5) Divide the dough into 5 to 6 equal parts and roll them into small balls (lime-sized).

6) Take one dough ball, cover with dry flour and roll it on a very lightly floured surface into a thin circle like a chapati, using a rolling pin on a board.

7) Apply ghee or oil liberally on the rolled disk, then spread ½ tsp of the spice mixture you made in step 1. Spread this spice mixture with your fingers. Now from the top of this chapati, start creating pleats by folding with the help of your fingers, held like a paper fan.

8) Dust some more dry flour on the folds and slightly stretch the pleated dough.

9) Begin to roll the pleated dough like a Swiss roll and secure the end by pressing gently.

10) Now take this 'Swill roll' ball, dust and roll out to a circle.

11) Heat a pan on a medium heat. When the pan is hot, put the rolled laccha paratha on it. Cook until the underside has brown spots (about 30 seconds), then grease the sides with oil.

12) Flip and roast both sides.

13) Then crush the paratha to form a layer.

14) Transfer the cooked paratha to a serving platter. Serve immediately, with the curry of your choice.

MAGICAL MUMBAI FLAVOURS

Indian Delicacies and Desserts

- *Masala Chai Crème Brûlée with Almond & Chocolate Madeleine*
- *Date Anjeer Barfi*
- *Vegan Aamrus Raspberry Cheesecake*
- *Almond Pistachio Cupcakes with Shrikhand Frosting*
- *Thandai Mousse Dome*
- *Pistachio Milk Chocolate Barfi Fudge*
- *Orange Chocolate Coconut Ladoo*
- *Shahi Tukda*

Masala Chai Crème Brûlée with Almond & Chocolate Madeleine

In India chai is more than just a cup of tea to start the day! There are various types of chai but my personal favourites are fresh ginger tea and masala chai (page 234). In those parts of India where coffee was not introduced, chai is where the morning begins, ideas flourish and work stops. The masala in masala chai is made with various spices like cardamom, cinnamon stick, cloves, black pepper, fennel seeds and ginger. The recipe differs from region to region and as per people's taste.

As I have mentioned before, I love creating fusion food and when I was thinking about desserts, I could not resist sharing the recipe for this masala chai crème brûlée and soft madeleines.

Madeleines are small sponge cakes from France baked in a shell-shaped mould. The bump on top of madeleines is very important as it's a sign of quality and is linked to well-controlled baking. There is a lot of debate about whether madeleines are cookies or cakes but for me, they taste amazing with either masala chai or masala chai crème brûlée.

Ingredients

(For chai masala (makes 1 cup))

8–10 green cardamom

2–3 black cardamom

2 tbsp black peppercorn

2 tbsp fennel seeds

8–9 cloves (*laung*)

2 inch cinnamon stick, broken

2 tsp dry ginger powder

1 star anise

¾ tsp nutmeg powder

A pinch of salt

(For crème brûlée (for 5–6 people))

400 ml of double cream or heavy cream

1-inch fresh ginger chopped

4 egg yolks

100 g white or brown sugar

2 tea bags or 1 tbsp loose tea

(For almond & chocolate madeleine: makes 10–12)

200 g all-purpose flour

225 g melted butter (melt the butter and set aside for 3 to 4 minutes)

50 g ground almond

A pinch of cardamom powder

100 g granulated sugar

1 tsp baking powder

1½ tbsp honey

A pinch of salt

3 eggs

Some chocolate buttons

(For decoration)

Tempered white chocolate

Some chopped pistachio

Dry rose petals

Instructions

For chai masala:

1) Dry-roast all the spices for 2 to 3 minutes on a low heat. Put them aside and let the mixture cool down for 10 minutes.

2) When the mixture has cooled down, grind to a powder and put it aside.

For crème brûlée:

3) Add double cream or heavy cream to a pot on a low heat. Add 2 tea bags (or 1 tbsp loose tea) to it. Add chopped fresh ginger to it. Let the mixture boil on a medium heat.

4) Once it starts boiling, add 1 tsp chai masala and mix. Let it boil for a minute or so on a low heat.

5) Turn off the hob and let the mixture cool down.

6) Take a bowl and add 4 egg yolk and sugar and beat until light and creamy about 2 to 3 minutes.

7) Now strain the boiled creamy chai into the egg and sugar mixture.

8) Mix everything together.

9) Take 4–5 ramekins and pour the chai mixture evenly.

10) Take a baking tray and place these ramekins in it. Pour enough boiling water into the baking tray to reach halfway up the sides of the ramekins.

11) Bake at a temperature of 140°C for 35 to 45 minutes.

12) Get the ramekins out and let them cool down for an hour. Then put them in the fridge for 2 hours or so, or up to two days.

13) Get sugar and cinnamon mixture ready (5–6 tbsp sugar and 1 tsp cinnamon powder).

14) When ready to serve, evenly sprinkle the sugar and cinnamon mixture so it covers the surface.

15) Carefully caramelise with a kitchen blowtorch or,

16) If you don't have a blowtorch, simply place the ramekins directly under the oven broiler, and carefully watch the sugar burn and form that glorious golden topping.

For madeleine:

17) Beat the egg and sugar together on high speed, with a handheld or standing mixer with a whisk attachment, for at least 5–6 minutes. Add ground almond, cardamom powder and honey and beat them until well combined.

18) Sift flour, baking powder and salt into this mixture. Combine with a whisk. Gently fold into egg mixture. Add melted butter and combine together. The batter will be thick, silky and shiny.

19) Transfer the mixture to a piping bag and refrigerate overnight. (I refrigerate mine for 24 hours)

20) Preheat the oven to 220°C. Butter the cavities of the madeleine mould and dust it with some flour (if you are using a metal madeleine mould as I do).

21) Take your madeleine mixture piping bag out of the fridge and fill the cavities up to half and add a chocolate button. And then add a tiny bit of madeleine mixture up to ¾ of the mould.

22) Bake your madeleines at 200°C for 4 minutes. Then turn the temperature down to 160°C and continue baking the madeleines for 6 to 8 minutes.

23) Take the mould tray out and let it cool down for 2 minutes or so. Then take the madeleines out one by one, with the help of a spoon.

24) Once your madeleines have cooled down, dip them in tempered white chocolate and add some chopped pistachios and rose petals.

Date Anjeer (Fig) Barfi
(can be made vegan)

India is a country of festivals and festivals are also the time when Indians prepare traditional Indian delicacies at home. Date anjeer barfi was one of the popular barfis in the Sharma household. My mum used to add some sugar and milk powder so that they looked and tasted like barfis bought from *mithai* (Indian sweet) shop.

The date anjeer barfi recipe I am sharing here is my all-time favourite because it is easy to make and is healthy without any added sugar. These barfi pieces are loaded with nuts too. Perfect to satisfy your sweet craving and you don't feel guilty after eating a barfi piece. Dates are great to make desserts, smoothies and even chutneys. They are naturally sweet and a great source of iron. This barfi is great for digestion and building your guts. I have added nuts like cashews, almonds, pistachios and walnuts, not just for the crunchiness but also for their health benefits as they provide healthy fats, fibres and protein.

Ingredients (makes 8–10 barfi rolls)

9–10 pitted dates

15–16 dry figs, soaked for at least 2 hours

¼ cup or handful of cashews, finely chopped

¼ cup or handful of almonds, finely chopped

¼ cup or handful of pistachios, finely chopped

¼ cup or handful of walnuts, finely chopped

1 tbsp dry rose petals

6–8 saffron strings

¼ tsp cardamom powder

3 tbsp poppy seeds

3 tbsp vegan butter or ghee or unsalted butter

Instructions

1) Grind pitted dates to paste. Please don't add any water while grinding.

2) In the same way, grind figs without water and make a paste.

3) Take a pan and, on a low heat, roast poppy seeds for 2 to 3 minutes. Keep stirring to save poppy seeds to burn. Put them aside.

4) In the same pan add 1 tbsp vegan butter or ghee or unsalted butter and roast all nuts for 2 to 3 minutes on a low heat. Put these nuts aside.

5) In the same pan, add 2 tbsp vegan butter or ghee or unsalted butter. Add date paste and fig paste. Keep stirring on a low heat. Cook until there is no moisture and when you move the mixture in a pan it moves from one side to another. The whole process takes 10 to 12 minutes.

6) Add roasted dry fruits, rose petals, saffron strands, cardamom powder and 1 tbsp roasted poppy seeds. Mix everything together.

7) Turn off the hob and let the mixture cool down at room temperature.

8) After 30 minutes or so, put some butter or ghee in your palm and roll it to make a small cylinder.

9) Wrap in a foil and put that in the fridge for 2 hours or so.

10) Add some poppy seeds to a tray or plate. Take the date and fig cylinder roll out of the fridge. Cover this roll with poppy seeds.

11) Cut these cylinder rolls into small pieces and serve.

Vegan Aamrus Raspberry Cheesecake

Aamrus is a popular seasonal sweet dish made from mango pulp and is eaten with pooris or chapatis. This traditional mango delicacy is popular in the Western Indian states of Maharashtra and Gujarat. I have used Alphonso mangos for this recipe but if these are not easily available you can use any mango or mango pulp available in your area.

Ingredients (makes enough for 6–8 people)

(For base layer)

120 g almond

60 g pistachio

10–12 pitted dates

60 g walnut

1 tsp vanilla extract

Pinch of salt

1 tbsp coconut cream (optional)

(For aamrus (mango) layer)

250 g cashews, soaked for at least 2 hours

130 ml mango purée

¼ tsp cardamom powder

A pinch of saffron strands

2 tbsp agar agar

¼ cup honey or maple syrup

(For raspberry layer)

120 g fresh raspberries or frozen raspberries

100 g jaggery, brown or white sugar

1½ tbsp agar agar

250 ml water

Some fresh raspberries, strawberries, mango chunks, mint leaves and blueberries for garnishing

Instructions

For base layer:

1) Take a food processor, add almond, pistachio and walnut and process until it forms a coarse crumble. Now add pitted dates, vanilla extract and a pinch of salt. Process until everything is well combined.

2) Line a cake tin, scoop the mixture into the cake tin and press it down to create a firm even base.

3) Put this in the fridge for 20 minutes or so.

For mango layer:

4) Drain off the water of cashews, add them to a food processor with mango purée, honey or maple syrup and make a smooth purée.

5) Take a pan and add 100ml water and agar agar. Mix them together and cook for 30–40 seconds on a medium heat. Add the mango purée you made in step 4 with this agar agar water and cook for 30 -40 seconds on a medium heat.

6) Turn off the hob and let the mixture cool down for 20 minutes or so.

7) Pour this mixture into a base layer. Put the cake tin in the fridge for at least 2 hours.

For raspberry layer:

8) Take a saucepan, add raspberries and sugar. Cook for 2 to 3 minutes on a medium heat. Turn the heat off. Let it cool down and blend it to a purée.

9) Take a pan, add 100 ml water and agar agar, Mix them together and cook for 30–40 seconds. Add raspberry purée, and cook for 3 to 4 minutes until the purée becomes slightly thick.

10) Once it cools down, pour on the top of the mango cashews layer.

11) Put the cake tin in the fridge for 2 hours.

12) Take the cake out of the tin and add some fresh strawberries, raspberries, mint leaves, mango chunks and blue berries for garnishing before you serve.

Almond Pistachio Cupcakes with Shrikhand Frosting

Shrikhand is one of the oldest desserts in India and is made of strained yoghurt or hung curd or *chakka*. It's a very popular dessert in Gujarat, Maharashtra and some parts of Madhya Pradesh. The name Shrikhand is derived from the Sanskrit word *Shikharini* which means a curd prepared with added sugar, nuts and fruits. If sweetened and flavoured hung curd or strained yoghurt doesn't sound like a dessert to you, I must point out that shrikhand is a must-have dessert in Maharashtrian and Gujarati weddings.

Would you believe cakes weren't popular in India a few decades ago? But now cakes are immensely popular in metropolitan cities like Mumbai, Delhi, Calcutta and Noida, just to name a few. If you wander around the rural areas of India, cakes are not common at all.

The whole purpose of sharing this recipe is to showcase how, when a 100-year-old traditional dessert engages with a western recipe, a truly luscious cupcake called almond pistachio cupcake with shrikhand frosting is created. I do hope you love this recipe and trust me, it doesn't take a long time.

Ingredients (4 people)

(For frosting)

500 g thick Greek yoghurt

1 cup powdered sugar

A pinch of saffron strands

½ tsp green cardamom powder

(For almond pistachio cupcakes)

120 g all-purpose flour or self-rising flour

60 g ground almond

30 g ground pistachio

110 g brown sugar or white sugar

2 pinches of salt

1½ tsp baking powder

125 g melted butter

½ tsp vanilla essence

2 large eggs

1 pinch of saffron soaked in ¼ cup warm milk

Instructions

1) Take a large bowl and place a strainer over it.

2) On top of the strainer, spread a thin muslin cloth or a cheese cloth.

3) Now pour the Greek yoghurt or curd into the bowl.

4) Wrap the yoghurt/curd in the cloth and gently squeeze to drain the excess way. Please don't squeeze hard, though!

5) Now place a heavy object on top of the cloth and place it in the fridge for 30 minutes so that all the excess whey comes out.

6) Now, take another bowl and add the drained yoghurt/hung curd and add saffron, powder sugar and cardamom or *elaichi* powder. Mix everything together.

7) Now take a piping bag, fill it with the shrikhand and keep it in the fridge. It can stay in the fridge for three to four days.

8) Preheat the oven to 180°C for 15 minutes and place cupcake liners in muffin pans.

9) In a bowl, crack eggs and add sugar. Whisk until fluffy and smooth. Add melted butter, sift all-purpose flour/self-raising flour, add baking powder, ground almond and pistachio and beat until nice and smooth.

10) Add salt, vanilla essence, and soaked saffron with milk. Mix everything together with a spatula. Please make sure there are no lumps.

11) Fill cupcake liners two-thirds full and bake until golden brown (about 15 to 20 minutes, depending on your oven). To check on progress, insert a toothpick: if it all comes out clear, your cupcakes are cooked.

12) Transfer the cupcakes to a wire rack and leave to cool.

13) Get your shrikhand frosting out and decorate your cupcakes. I have added some chopped pistachio, saffron strands, dry rose petals and edible silver foil on the top.

Thandai Mousse Dome

Thandai: a traditional, milk-based Indian drink which I drink on every holiday. Thandai is believed to be a favourite drink of Lord Shiva. It is believed to have been first used in India around 1000 BC. Thandai is a summer drink in north Indian regions, where it is an instant energy drink in the scorching summer heat.

I have taken this thandai one step further and created an easy mousse dome. I made them colourful: as I mentioned before, thandai is enjoyed during India's Festival of Colours.

Ingredients

(For thandai powder mix (1 cup) – you can keep this mixture for at least 2 months in an airtight jar)

30 g almonds

30 g pistachios

30 g cashews

1 tbsp poppy seeds

2 tsp fennel seeds

1 tbsp melon seed or *magaz*

1 tbsp peppercorns

¼ tsp nutmeg powder

A pinch of saffron

8–10 cardamom pods

1 tbsp dry rose petals

(For mousse dome)

250 ml double cream or heavy cream for making thandai

350 ml whipped cream

1½ tbsp thandai masala

75 g white grated chocolate

> **TIPS:**
> a) When making thandai masala, please do not grind for too long, as the nuts will start releasing their essential oil and the fine powder will become paste-like.
> b) If you don't find whipped cream, you can make whipped cream by using double cream or heavy cream. Whisk until you get stiff peaks.

Instructions

For thandai masala:

1) Grind all the ingredients mentioned in "for thandai powder mix" to a coarsely ground powder. Please do not add any water. Grind this mixture in intervals.

For mousse dome:

2) Heat a pan on a medium heat, add 250 ml double cream and add thandai masala. Mix and infuse double cream with thandai masala.

3) Take a pan part-filled with water, sit a glass bowl on the water in the pan and add grated white chocolate. Temper for 3 to 4 minutes.

4) Add thandai double cream to tempered chocolate. And mix everything well until you get a smooth mixture.

5) Now add whipped cream in batches and fold.

6) Take a silicon mould tray and sprinkle some edible colour of your choice or paint.

7) Add thandai mousse mixture to these moulds. Please don't fill moulds to the top.

8) Put the tray in the freezer for at least 3 hours.

9) Serve with thandai hot milk, or on their own.

Pistachio Milk Chocolate Barfi Fudge

This is an easy-to-make recipe and it tastes heavenly.

Ingredients

100 g ghee or unsalted butter

100 ml milk

200 g milk powder

100 ml condensed milk

150 g white chocolate, grated

30 g ground pistachio

½ tsp cardamom powder

3–4 tbsp sugar (optional)

Few edible flowers and edible silver leaf for garnishing

Instructions

1) Heat a pan on a medium heat. Add ghee and milk. Stir and cook for 2 minutes. Now add milk powder, condensed milk, milk chocolate, ground pistachio and sugar.

2) Keep stirring until the mixture is smooth and firm (around 10–12 minutes). Turn the hob off.

3) Pour the fudge mixture into a greased tray covered with butter paper.

4) When this mixture has partially cooled down, decorate with edible flowers, pistachios and silver leaf.

5) Let it set for 2–3 hours.

6) Cut into desired shapes.

Orange Chocolate Coconut Ladoo

Ladoo – another one of the oldest sweet dishes in India which you enjoy on every auspicious occasion as an expression of blessing and joy. But they were once used as medicine by an ancient Indian physician, Susrutha, in the fourth century BC. There is no single way to prepare them. There are various kinds of ladoos, differing from region to region and having their unique taste. My personal favourite ladoos are motichur ladoo which my nan used to make when we as a family visited her and orange chocolate ladoo because I just love the combination of orange chocolate with coconut.

These ladoos are very easy to make and are small, sweet treats for you and your loved ones.

Ingredients (15–16 ladoos)

½ tsp ghee

175 g fine desiccated coconut (fine)

100 ml condensed milk

50 g orange chocolate (tempered)

A pinch of cardamom powder

3 tbsp desiccated coconut (for garnishing)

Pistachios for garnishing (optional)

> **TIP:** If desiccated coconut is coarse, please blend it in the mixer grinder for a few seconds.

Instructions

1) Heat ghee in a pan on a low to medium heat. Add fine desiccated coconut and condensed milk and stir for 2 to 3 minutes. Now add tempered orange chocolate and ground cardamom. Mix everything together.

2) Turn off the hob and let the mixture cool down for a few minutes.

3) Spread some ghee between your palms. Take a small portion of this mixture and roll into balls.

4) Roll these coconut chocolate balls in dry desiccated coconut immediately and attach a pistachio to every ladoo.

Shahi Tukda

This is a classic, rich (or *shahi*), sweet Indian dessert which hails from the streets of Delhi. And if you are in Delhi, you cannot miss street hawkers selling this mouth-watering Indian version of British classic bread and butter pudding. My favourite place to enjoy the real shahi tukda is a place called *Shahi tukda* near Jama Masjid, Delhi.

Shahi tukda is a rich dessert made with fried bread, ghee, sugar, milk and nuts. This royal dessert is said to have originated during the Mughal empire and was enjoyed as Iftar meals during the month of Ramadan.

Ingredients (3 people)

4 medium size bread slices (cut in triangle shapes)

100 g sugar

100 ml water

2 medium size bread (for breadcrumbs)

2 tbsp ghee or unsalted butter

450 ml full-fat milk

100 g milk powder

3 tbsp sugar

A generous pinch of saffron strands

¼ tsp ground cardamom

A drop of rose essence or rose water

30 g chopped cashews and pistachios

Instructions

1)   Brush melted ghee or butter on both sides of triangle-shaped bread slices. Be generous to spread butter on these slices.

2)   Heat a pan on a low heat and toast the slices until they are golden brown. Please don't be tempted to toast the slices on a high flame.

3)   Take a milk pan, add 100 g sugar and 100 ml water. Mix everything together and cook until sugar dissolves. Please do keep stirring.

4)   Let the mixture cool down for 2 to 3 minutes. Now add shallow fried bread slices (one at a time) and make sure they are covered with this sugar mixture. Keep them in a tray.

5)   Take 2 slices of bread. Cut the crust of the bread slices. Use a mixer grinder and grind them to breadcrumbs.

6) Take a pan and heat milk with milk powder. Keep stirring and boil until there are no lumps (approximately 4 to 5 minutes) on a medium to high heat. Add freshly made breadcrumbs, sugar, chopped nuts, saffron and a drop of rose essence or rose water. Keep stirring until milk thickens and becomes a yellow(ish) colour on a low heat.

7) Now add 1 tsp ghee or unsalted butter and ground cardamom.

8) Now pour the mixture on sugar syrup coated bread slices (Step 4) and if possible, cover the slices with the milk mixture.

9) Decorate with some chopped dry fruits and rose petals.

Sides and Chutneys

Whole Moong and Baby Potatoes Salad

Ingredients (2 people)

200 g whole moong (or mung) bean (soaked overnight)

6–8 baby potatoes, boiled and halved

1 small tomato, finely chopped

½ cup yoghurt, optional

1 small red onion, finely chopped

50 g avocado cubes, optional

30 g seedless olives

½ cucumber, roughly chopped

¼ tsp black pepper, ground

1 tbsp lemon juice

Salt to taste

2 pinches of chaat masala (see page 241)

2 tbsp olive oil

Instructions

1) Heat 2 tbsp oil in a pan on a medium heat. When the oil is hot, add boiled and halved potatoes. Add a pinch of salt and sauté them for 3 to 4 minutes. add soaked and drained moong beans. Add 2 tbsp water and a pinch of salt. Mix everything well, put the lid on and let moong beans cook for 2 to 3 minutes.

2) Turn off the hob and let moong beans and potatoes cool down.

3) In a bowl, add chopped onions, tomatoes, avocado, cucumber and all the other ingredients. Mix everything well and then add cooked moong beans.

4) This moong potato salad is ready to eat. You can either serve it as a side dish while eating your lunch or dinner or eat it on its own.

Apple Beetroot Chutney

Ingredients (makes 1 cup)

2 apples (pink lady or royal gala, skinned and chopped)

1 boiled beetroot, chopped

2 inches of ginger, chopped

½ tsp cumin seeds

100 g sugar

1 tsp lemon juice

¼ tsp chilli powder (optional)

½ tsp cinnamon powder or 1 inch cinnamon stick

Salt to taste

½ tsp garam masala

¼ cup water

Instructions

1) Heat a pan on a medium heat. Add chopped apples, sugar, water, lemon juice, chopped ginger, cumin seeds and cinnamon. Put the lid on and cook on a low heat until the apples are soft (approximately 10 to 15 minutes).

2) Now add chopped beetroot, chilli powder and garam masala. Cook for a further 2 minutes.

3) Turn off the hob and let the mixture cool down. Transfer the mixture to a blender and blend it into a chunky chutney, or you can blend it really fine. Taste before you serve.

Mint and Coriander Chutney

Ingredients (makes ½ cup)

30 g fresh mint leaves

60 g fresh coriander leaves, with stem

½ tsp chaat masala (page 241)

2 garlic cloves

½ inch ginger

1–2 green chill

½ tsp lemon juice

Salt to taste

Instructions

1) Take a blender and add the ingredients to it. Add 2–3 ice cubes and a ¼ cup of water and salt. Grind everything and your chutney is ready. Taste before you use it.

TIP: When you add ice cubes while grinding, they maintain the temperature and save the mint and coriander from going darker in colour.

Red Garlic Chutney

Ingredients (makes ½ cup)

4 tbsp desiccated coconut

2 tbsp peanuts (optional)

1 tbsp sesame seeds (optional)

4 dry red chillies (Kashmiri or bydgi)

5 -6 garlic cloves, peeled

½ tsp chilli powder

Salt to taste

Instructions

1) Heat a non-stick pan over a medium heat. Add desiccated coconut and dry roast for 30 seconds or so. Keep stirring desiccated coconut to stop it from burning.

2) Transfer the roasted desiccated coconut onto a plate and set aside to cool.

3) In the same pan, add the peanuts and roast them until golden. Transfer them onto the same plate and set aside.

4) In the same pan, add dried red chillies and sesame seeds and roast them until golden. Transfer them onto the same plate.

5) Now add the garlic cloves to the same pan and sauté for 1 minute.

6) Once all the roasted ingredients have cooled down, transfer them to a spice blender along with some salt and red chilli powder and grind them to a dry coarse chutney.

Sweet Chilli Red Pepper Chutney

Ingredients (makes 1 cup)

2 red peppers (chopped)

2–4 red fresh chillies, chopped
(as per your taste)

50 g sugar or 50 g brown sugar

100 ml white wine vinegar

Salt to taste

Instructions:

1) Blend chopped pepper and red chillies.

2) Heat vinegar and sugar in a pan on a medium heat. When sugar is dissolved in vinegar, add blended chopped pepper and red chillies.

3) Cook for 10–12 minutes on a low heat.

4) Turn off the hob. Let the mixture cool down.

5) This chutney goes really well with any finger food and pakoras.

Schezwan or Sichuan Chutney

Ingredients

15 to 18 red dry chillies (deseeded if you want it less spicy)

12 to 10 garlic cloves, finely chopped

1 inch ginger, peeled and finely chopped

1 small red onion, finely chopped

3 tbsp sesame oil or any cooking oil for cooking

2 tbsp oil for mixing at a later stage

½ tsp black pepper, ground

½ tsp light soy sauce

1 tbsp white vinegar or lemon juice

1 tbsp paprika

1½ tbsp tomato ketchup

1 tsp sugar

Salt to taste

Instructions

1) Remove stems from dry red chillies. Cut chillies into halves and remove seeds. Soak chillies in warm water for 30 minutes.

2) After 30 minutes, drain excess water from red chillies and transfer them to a small grinding jar. Add 2 tbsp water and grind the chillies to a thick smooth paste.

3) Heat a pan on a medium heat and add oil. When the oil is hot, add chopped garlic and ginger. Sauté and cook for 2 minutes.

4) Now add finely chopped onions and sauté for 5 to 6 minutes until the onions are translucent.

5) Add ground chilli paste, soy sauce, vinegar, ground black pepper, tomato ketchup, sugar, paprika and salt to taste. Mix everything well.

6) Now mix ½ a cup of water and cook for a further 3 to 4 minutes.

7) Add 2 more tbsp oil and mix well. (This will work as a natural preservative

8) Turn off the hob and let the mixture cool down.

9) Once the mixture has cooled down, transfer it to a container or a jar and leave it in the fridge to use at any time. This chutney should be fine for at least 2 weeks.

Prune, Date and Tamarind Chutney

Ingredients

5–6 prunes (deseeded)

8–10 Dates (soft pitted dates)

1 inch (tamarind slab)

½ cup jaggery, grated

½ tsp chilli powder

1 tsp cumin seeds powder

Salt to taste

Instructions

1) Take a pan and add prunes, dates, tamarind, jaggery and 1½ cups of water. Boil this mixture on a high heat.

2) When the water starts boiling, reduce the heat to low and add salt, cumin powder and chilli powder.

3) Cook for a further 10 minutes. Turn off the hop and let the mixture cool down completely.

4) Blend in a mixer to a smooth, slightly runny chutney. If necessary, you can add water. Strain the chutney using a strainer.

5) Use as required and store the remaining in an airtight container in a fridge. It can be frozen for 3 months.

Koshimbir Raita

Ingredients

1 small cucumber (finely chopped)

1 tomato (finely chopped)

1 red onion (finely chopped)

1 -2 fresh green chillies (finely chopped)

Handful coriander (finely chopped)

Salt to taste

½ tsp Chaat masala (page 241)

250g plain yoghurt

Instructions

1) Take a bowl and mix finely chopped cucumber, tomato, red onion, chillies and coriander. Add plain yoghurt, salt and chat masala and mix everything together

2) Serve with biryani, pilau dishes or with any curry dishes.

Indian Teas

Ginger tea

Ingredients (for 4 people)

300 ml water

4 breakfast tea bags or 1½ tsp loose tea

2 inches of ginger, washed and crushed

3–4 black peppercorns

Sugar (as per your choice)

Milk (as per your choice)

Instructions

1) Add 300 ml water to a pan. Heat this pan on a high heat. Add crushed ginger and black peppercorn and let this water boil.

2) When it's boiling, add sugar and tea bags or loose tea. Put the lid on and let the tea boil for another 2 to 3 minutes on a low heat.

3) Turn the hob off, let the tea settle down for a few seconds, pour tea into your cup using a strainer, add milk if you want to and enjoy with your favourite biscuits or madeleines (page 203).

Masala Chai

Ingredients (for 2 people)

150 ml water

2 tea bags or 1 tsp loose tea

½ inch ginger, washed and crushed

150 ml milk

½ tsp chai masala (page 204)

Sugar as per your choice

Instructions

1) Add a cup of water to a pan. Heat this pan on a high heat. Add ginger, milk and tea bags or loose tea. Let it boil.

2) When it starts boiling, add chai masala and cook for a minute or so on a low to medium heat.

3) Pour in your cup with the help of a strainer.

4) Enjoy with biscuits of your choice, madeleines or pakoras.

Masala Recipes

Garam Masala

Garam masala is one of the important ingredients in Indian cooking. There is no set recipe for garam masala, as the recipe varies greatly from region to region and as per your personal preference. *Garam* means 'hot' and *masala* means 'a mixture of spices'. So, garam masala is a blend of some spices that add warmth and flavour to your food but doesn't make your food spicy.

A lot of time, I do get asked – are curry powder and garam masala the same? The answer to that question is no.

In Indian cooking, there is no such thing as curry or curry powder. Since childhood, I had a friend from Tamil Nadu (the southern part of India) who always used to say the word *kaari* in her language. Her family was *Brahmin* and they always used to call their vegetable dishes *kaari*: these used to be cooked with spices and some coconut paste. But on the other hand, Tamil people who eat meat dishes use the same word, but they pronounce it with more emphasis on the end of the word, as in *kaaree*.

The word 'curry' was given by the British Raj when they encountered various spicy gravy dishes in India. My great-granddad used to say that an Indian spice merchant invented the well-known curry powder for British colonial personnel returning to Britain. Curry powder is a generic mix of Indian spices like coriander seeds, cumin seeds, turmeric, nutmeg, cloves, bay leaf, onion powder and black peppercorn. It works well if you are adding it as a spice blend for your dishes, but it does not give that authentic flavour. You can use supermarket-bought curry powder if you are in hurry or you are a new learner. My personal favourite is freshly made garam masala as it gives that unique taste, and it does not take that long.

I do hope you find the following recipe for garam masala helpful.

Ingredients (makes 1 cup)

30 g green coriander seeds

3 tbsp cumin seeds

1 tbsp shahi jeera

1 tsp fennel seeds

5–6 green cardamom

5–6 cloves

2–3 black cardamom

1 inch stone flower

2-inch cinnamon stick

2 tbsp black peppercorn

1 star anise

1–2 whole Kashmir red chillies

1 mace

1 bay leaf

Salt to taste

Instructions

1) Heat a pan on a low heat. When pan is hot, add coriander seeds. Roast them lightly for 2 to 3 minutes. Keep stirring them. Remove and put them aside.

2) Now in the same pan add cumin seeds, fennel seeds and shahi jeera. Roast them lightly and put aside to cool down. (You can add these on top of the roasted coriander seeds.)

3) Now in the same pan add all the other remaining spices and salt. Roast them until the spices are fragrant.

4) Remove them and combine them with roasted coriander, cumin seeds and shahi jeera. Let the mixture cool down completely.

5) Take a spice blender and make sure the jar is completely dry. Add the spices to a blender and blend to a fine powder. Store this freshly made garam masala in an airtight container.

TIP: Salt helps maintain and keep the fragrance of the spices once they are ground.

Pastes

Garlic Paste

Ingredients

300 g Garlic

1 tsp salt

Water (if needed)

Instructions

1) Peel off garlic cloves (please see page 18 for ways to peel).
2) Take a blender and add peeled garlic cloves and 1 tsp salt and grind this to a thick paste.
3) You can add a splash of water if needed.
4) Put this paste into a mason jar or similar airtight container. Once in the fridge, this garlic paste should be used within 4 months.

Ginger Paste

Ingredients

300 g ginger

1 tsp salt

Water (if needed)

Instructions

1) Peel off ginger (please see page 19 for ways to peel).
2) Take a blender and add peeled ginger and 1 tsp salt and grind this to a thick paste.
3) You can add a splash of water if needed.
4) Put this paste into a mason jar or similar airtight container. Once in the fridge, this ginger paste should be used within 4 months.

Pav Bhaji Masala

Ingredients

3 tbsp coriander seeds

1 tsp fennel seeds

3 tsp cumin seeds

1 inch cinnamon stick

1 bay leaf

2 black cardamom

8–9 cloves

2 star anise

1 tbsp black peppercorn

7–8 whole red Kashmiri chillies or bedgyi chillies

1 tbsp dry fenugreek leaves or kasuri methi (optional)

1 mace or javitri flower or ½ tsp mace powder (optional)

5–6 green cardamoms

1 tsp dry mango powder

2 tsp dry ginger powder

1 tsp dry garlic powder

½ tsp turmeric powder

½ tsp chilli powder

1 tsp black salt or normal salt

PLEASE NOTE –
a) if you don't have whole red chillies, you can substitute that with 1.5 tsp chilli powder and add it when you are adding turmeric powder.
b) If you can't get dry ginger powder and dry garlic powder, you can skip this stage. Instead, you can add fresh ginger and garlic by grinding 1 inch of ginger and 3 to 4 garlic cloves with pav bhaji masala. It will still give you that flavour.

Instructions

1)   Heat a pan on a low heat. Add coriander seeds, black peppercorn, cloves, star anise, cumin seeds, fennel seeds, cinnamon stick and black cardamom. Roast them for 5–6 minutes. Keep stirring and make sure none of these whole spices get burnt. Remove and put them aside.

2)   In the same pan add red chillies and bay leaves. Roast them for 3 to 4 minutes. Remove and combine them with the other mixture you roasted in step 1. Let the mixture cool down completely.

3) Now add turmeric powder, black salt or normal salt, dry mango powder, dry garlic powder, dry ginger powder, mace or mace powder, green cardamom and dry fenugreek leaves. Mix everything together.

4) Take a spice blender. And make sure the jar is completely dry. Now grind the spices to a fine powder.

5) Now sieve the pav phaji masala powder to remove any coarse particles. Grind the coarse particles again and sieve.

6) Let the mixture cool down completely and store in an airtight container. This freshly made masala can stay fresh for 6 months.

Chaat Masala

Chaat means 'lick' and is used as a topping on snacks, appetizers and finger food. When you are on the streets of Mumbai enjoying the street food, you will come across this essential masala. Yes, I am saying 'essential' because the sprinkle of this tangy spice blend perks up the flavours of masala toast, raita, Mexican aloo chaat, aloo chaat and all the starters, snacks and street food mentioned in this book.

Ingredients

30 g cumin seeds or jeera

15 g black peppercorns

1 tbsp dry mango powder or amchur

1 tbsp dry ginger powder

½ tsp Kashmiri chilli powder (optional)

Handful mint leaves

2½ tbsp black salt powder

2 tbsp sea salt

½ tsp asafoetida

Instructions

1) Heat a pan on a low heat and add cumin seeds and dry roast on a medium flame for a minute or so. Keep stirring them and make sure they go brownish and not black. (If they go very dark or black in colour, the cumin seeds will taste bitter.)

2) Remove cumin seeds, putting them in a bowl. Allow them to cool.

3) Dry roast black peppercorns for 30 seconds or so and add them to the same bowl.

4) Dry roast sea salt for a minute or so. Now add asafoetida, ginger powder and dry mango powder/amchur to the sea salt and mix them in. Keep stirring the mixture for 30–40 seconds. (The reason for roasting spices with salt is to evaporate the moisture from the mixture.)

5) Transfer the mixture to the bowl and add chilli powder.

6) Now dry roast mint leaves until they become dry, the green colour starts fading away and they become crunchy. Please do keep stirring the leaves so that they don't get burnt.

7) Now transfer the dried mint leaves with other ingredients to a bowl and let the whole mixture cool down (30 to 40 minutes).

8) Once the mixture has cooled down completely, add black salt powder and mix.

9) In a spice blender, grind the spice mixture into a fine powder.

10) Store it in an airtight container away from direct heat. This chaat masala will be fine for at least 6 months if stored properly.

PLEASE NOTE:
If you are out of India, you can easily buy black salt, dry or raw mango powder (amchur) and dry ginger powder from many Indian shops, or you can buy them online.